ONE-MINUTE
PRAYERS®
for Those with
CANCER

NICK HARRISON

HARVEST HOUSE PUBLISHERS
EUGENE, OREGON

One-Minute Prayers® for Those with Cancer
Copyright © 2018 by Nick Harrison
Published by Harvest House Publishers
Eugene, Oregon 97408
www.harvesthousepublishers.com

ISBN 978-0-7369-7274-1 (pbk.)
ISBN 978-0-7369-7275-8 (eBook)

Printed in China

18 19 20 21 22 23 24 25 26 / RDS-SK / 10 9 8 7 6 5 4 3 2 1

INTRODUCTION

If you're holding this book, I presume you're one of the nearly 15 million Americans presently diagnosed with cancer. No doubt about it, cancer is epidemic these days. A few years ago the President's Cancer Panel reported that 41 percent of Americans will be diagnosed with cancer during their lifetime. Such a large company of fellow travelers, and yet when we hear the words, "It's cancer," we somehow feel alone, separated from our friends and relatives who remain cancer free. In short, we belong to a club we did not ask to join.

The good news is that, according to the American Cancer Society, the death rate from cancer has decreased 25 percent since 1991, which means 2.1 million deaths were averted during those years. Cancer *is* survivable. Early detection is an important factor. So is the chosen protocol recommended by your oncologist.

But another often overlooked factor is *prayer*. That's what this book is about. These short prayers are designed to help you along the way on your cancer journey, whether you've been recently diagnosed or whether cancer has become a longtime, recurring companion.

One factor many of those with cancer have found helpful is forming a support team. This is a group of trusted people who will be pulling for you, possibly advising you, helping out with practical matters when needed, and, of course, praying for you. I suggest your support team include your medical advisers (oncologist, primary care doctor, and perhaps a nutritionist), a few close family members, praying friends, your pastor, and acquaintances who are cancer survivors themselves.

As you proceed through your cancer treatment, keep your team informed, solicit their advice (but always seek confirmation from your medical advisers), and tell them your specific prayer (and practical) needs. Let them help shoulder the burden, just as the four friends of the paralytic in Mark 2:1-5 became a support team by lowering their friend through the roof into the presence of Jesus, who then healed the man (verses 11-12).

I, too, would like to be on your support team as one who is praying for you. As this book is published, please know that I'm praying for every reader to overcome their fears, wisely choose the best treatments, and most of all trust God with the outcome.

You might ask, *How can short one-minute prayers accomplish much in my fight against cancer?* My reply is that the effectiveness of true prayer is not dependent on its length. Plus, my hope is that these prayers will serve as a jump-start to your own prayers. As you conclude a prayer on each page, I hope you'll add your own heartfelt words for as long as they continue to come. Prayer can accomplish much!

A personal example of this is my mother, who was diagnosed with ovarian cancer. She decided to forgo surgery and opted for chemotherapy. As we prayed for her, Mom's oncologist reported remarkable results. In fact, he used that very word—"remarkable"—to describe her improvement. Later, he ended her chemo treatments before the final scheduled session, saying that in all his years of treating cancer patients, he had never recommended such a decision before. Mom eventually did pass on from her cancer, but it was at age 92 and after the extra time God gave her through her successful chemo treatment and our prayers.

My own cancer was discovered early and dealt with through surgery. Again, there was much prayer on my part regarding my future. I well remember the early days of my diagnosis and the uncertainty I was facing. So, yes, I know the fear. I know the anxiety. I know the discomfort. I understand it all.

Before you begin, there are three things you should know about this book. First, the prayers are from a decidedly Christian perspective. That is, they are prayers for men and women who know their eternal destiny once they pass from this life, whether from cancer or from some other cause many years from now. If you have any uncertainty about your eternal destiny, I urge you, in childlike faith, to trust in Christ as your Lord and Savior now. The apostle Paul tells us in Romans 10:9, "If you confess with your mouth that Jesus is Lord and believe in your heart that God raised him from the dead, you will be saved." Once you have trusted in Christ, there is no need to fear death. You have his promise of eternal life, as recounted in the familiar words of John 3:16: "For God so loved the world, that he gave his only Son, that whoever believes in him should not perish but have eternal life." If you have believed in him, you will live even after you die.

Second, these prayers are for any person with cancer, no matter whether your prognosis is terminal or promising.

Third, since there are several common concerns we have as we face cancer, several themes are repeated in the following prayers. We're continually praying *against* fear, depression, and discouragement. We're praying *for* courage, strength, and—God willing—a return to good health.

You'll find that each page has a title theme at the top, followed by a relevant scripture, a reminder about the day's theme, and then the day's prayer.

I hope these prayers will open up a pathway of courage for you as you battle with cancer. God bless you as you walk the cancer path.

HOPE

*Surely there is a future, and your
hope will not be cut off.*
PROVERBS 23:18

When we hear the word "cancer" used in reference to us, it's a natural response to assume the worst. We wonder if our will is up to date, how we will tell those we love, and whether or not we will have much pain. How much time do we have?

Such worrying, though natural, is premature. In recent decades, the cancer survival rate has increased enormously. A cancer diagnosis is no longer a certain death sentence.

More importantly, God is in control. He sees your situation. He is with you now and will be with you through your treatment. Isn't that a great reason to hope? Make hope in God your anchor through your cancer journey.

Dear Lord, I need hope. I need to believe you surely have a future for me. I pray for the kind of hope only you can deliver. I pray for hopeful signs to come my way from those caring for me. In all that lies ahead, give me strength to endure and come out the other side of my treatment. This, Lord, is my earthly hope. But you, Lord, are my eternal hope.

You're on a Journey

*The LORD went before them by day in a pillar
of cloud to lead them along the way, and by
night in a pillar of fire to give them light, that
they might travel by day and by night.*

EXODUS 13:21

When the Israelites made their long, tiresome journey through a rough and unwelcoming land, God was with them...leading them...providing for them. Just as he does today for us as we travel through the desert of cancer.

God, I need a sheltering pillar of cloud along my way as I take this journey I did not choose. Lord, I need you to light my path with a pillar of fire during the darkest nights. Make the road ahead safe for me, as these are unknown paths I travel. Go before me in every aspect of my treatments. Give wisdom to my doctors and caregivers. Give patience to my family. May I have the necessary faith to take this journey and arrive safely on the other side of cancer. As I travel, I pray you'll introduce me to new companions on the journey—including others who are on the same long road. Bring us safely through, Lord.

ALLOW YOURSELF TO GRIEVE

*In this you rejoice, though now for a little while, if
necessary, you have been grieved by various trials.*
1 PETER 1:6

Cancer is a trial of the first order. Questions abound.
Anxiety looms. Emotions run high. One of those
emotions may be grief. We sense a loss, even when the
prognosis is favorable. We were healthy...and now we
are not. Our world shifts.

Please know that grief is a normal part of what
you're going through. Allow yourself time to grieve and
to process this turn of events. God understands.

God, I feel like I've momentarily lost my way. I've also
lost a form of happiness that came from being healthy.
In the midst of my trust in you, I still feel a profound
sense of grief at my diagnosis. Thank you for understanding how I feel. Even Jesus must have felt some
sense of grief when he prayed that if it were possible,
the cup of crucifixion might pass from him. I have a cup
in front of me—a cup from which I would prefer not to
drink. Still, as with Jesus, I accept your plan for my life.
I will grieve...and then I will move ahead with courage.

USED BY GOD

If anyone serves me, he must follow me; and
where I am, there will my servant be also. If
anyone serves me, the Father will honor him.

JOHN 12:26

We who are believers in Christ follow him wherever he leads—even into the chemo room. No matter what we are facing, we must be where our Father is and continue about his business.

Father, I'm your servant. I follow you wherever you lead. Right now, I follow you into a battle with cancer. Here I will learn much and experience suffering, but I will be in the company of Jesus, the one who suffered for me. I pray that in following you onto this battlefield, I will find a purpose in my present hardships. I pray that while I'm here, I will serve you as best I can. Show me how to honor you in the midst of cancer. Show me how I can be used by you during this time.

Questions and Answers

If any of you lacks wisdom, let him ask
God, who gives generously to all without
reproach, and it will be given him.
JAMES 1:5

A cancer diagnosis usually elicits several questions. Most often we ask, *Why me? Why now?* God's ways can be mysterious and beyond finding out. We may never know *why* something bad happens to us. However, at such questioning times, we can ask God for wisdom in how to handle our diagnosis, and he will answer day by day.

Lord, cancer is so rampant these days that I shouldn't be surprised it has come knocking on my door. Still, I wonder why I have to endure the suffering that cancer brings. So, Lord, I pray that you will help me understand what part this chapter in the book of my life will play in the story you've written for me. I pray that in understanding, I'll be more patient, and in gaining wisdom about my cancer, I'll know how to proceed wisely. Lord, please show me the way. Please impart wisdom generously.

Prayer as Medicine

Heal me, O Lord, and I shall be healed;
save me, and I shall be saved,
for you are my praise.
JEREMIAH 17:14

In our eagerness to hope that the current treatment for our cancer will be successful, we might overlook our greatest weapon in the cancer-fighting arsenal—prayer. We must keep asking, keep seeking, keep believing for God's hand in our healing. Keep prayer uppermost in your fight. Praise God if healing comes...and praise him if it doesn't. Remember to never blame yourself for "not praying hard enough." We may safely offer even small prayers, and they will be heard by our very big God.

Lord, I pray with Jeremiah, "Heal me...and I shall be healed." God, keep your faithful hand on my body. Bring health and healing to my bones. Lift my pain; help me to endure whatever lies ahead. You, Father, are my praise. You are the one I worship. You are the healer of my body and my soul. Strengthen me, Lord. Bring me great peace as I travel this journey. "Save me, and I shall be saved."

Praying for Your Support Team

By wise guidance you can wage your war,
and in abundance of counselors there is victory.
Proverbs 24:6

Your support team consists of all those who are helping you in your fight. That includes your doctors, chemo nurses, radiologists, family, friends, pastoral staff—any of those you've enlisted to aid you in your cancer battle. Pray for them often. Ask God to give them wisdom and to guide you effectively.

Father God, thank you for helping me assemble my support team. I pray for each member, considering them to be chosen by you to help me in my fight. May you give each of them wisdom. Help me listen when they offer me their objective counsel. May they not be afraid to be honest with me, even if the news isn't what I want to hear. At all times I pray they'll be my encouragers and in no way discourage me or bring me down. Help me be discerning when you bring a new team member my way. May each team member be chosen by you to guide me. And please, Lord, be the captain of my team.

Choosing Patience

I waited patiently for the LORD;
he inclined to me and heard my cry.
PSALM 40:1

Cancer is not usually eradicated quickly. After experiencing the symptoms, there are the tests, the consultation, and the diagnosis. Then there are the treatment options to be chosen. After that, there are the treatments themselves, some of which can be lengthy and accompanied by unpleasant side effects. After treatment, there are follow-up visits and often additional tests.

The ongoing trial can seem never ending. All the more reason to wait patiently for the Lord. He hears our cry.

Lord, you know my need of patience. Under normal circumstances, it's hard to endure waiting. Now, with cancer, it seems I'm always waiting for the next cancer-related event. Father, I pray for more patience. Help me to wait upon you. Lord, incline your ear to me. Hear my cry. Teach me not to be in such a hurry to get to tomorrow, causing me to miss the enjoyment of today.

SEEKING THE LORD

The afflicted shall eat and be satisfied;
those who seek him shall praise the LORD!
PSALM 22:26

W e're inclined to think it's easiest to seek and find God when everything is going well. But God loves to be sought when we're carrying an unbearable burden. In finding him, we find One who will remove the hopelessness of that burden. When we're afflicted, we can seek God, praise him, and be satisfied.

O Lord, I hunger for you. I hunger for your presence, your peace, and your power in my life. In you I find satisfaction for my soul, even as my body rebels against itself. Though I hate this cancer, I thank you that it causes me to seek you in an even greater way than when I was in good health. I pray that during the days of my affliction, I will turn to you, eat of you, and be fully satisfied—both spiritually and physically.

COOPERATING WITH GOD

His mother said to the servants,
"Do whatever he tells you."
JOHN 2:5

When Jesus was about to perform his first public miracle at the wedding at Cana by providing additional wine when the vats were empty, Mary instructed the servants to "do whatever he tells you." That's good advice 2,000 years later. Often God will direct us in how we should respond to life's challenges—even the challenge of cancer. Pray for God's leading, then follow it.

God, I know you have many ways of healing. You use doctors, you use nature's remedies, and you even heal supernaturally at times. I pray you'll help me know how to proceed in dealing with my cancer each step of the way. Instruct me in the way I should go, and I will follow. Advise me through my support team, through my doctors, or in any way you choose. Give me ears to hear and wise counselors to confirm the path I need to take.

Why Me, Lord?

*We know that for those who love God all
things work together for good, for those
who are called according to his purpose.*

ROMANS 8:28

Asking "Why me?" or "Why now?" is a natural response to a cancer diagnosis. The answer we receive is often stark silence. Crickets. But because God cannot lie, we know from his Word that even cancer can have a positive purpose. It *can* work together for our good. As we believe this, and as we trust God with our cancer, we may in time see God's answer to our questions. Trust and have patience.

God, if this cancer is meant to teach me something, couldn't I learn it some other way? I don't like being afraid of lab tests and chemo infusions and *waiting*. Yet I know you would have me walk by faith, and I do believe this cancer event will somehow work together for my good, even if I don't understand how that can be. Help me as I take each small step toward understanding your purpose in this trial. And may the good that comes from this journey in some way glorify you.

BUILDING UP YOUR
IMMUNE SYSTEM

*I praise you, for I am fearfully and
wonderfully made. Wonderful are your
works; my soul knows it very well.*
PSALM 139:14

Part of God's marvelous design for us is our immune system, which wards off illnesses from colds to cancer—when it's working right. In our fight against cancer, building up our immune system can be a big help. We do this through proper nutrition, exercise, prayer, and sometimes through nutritional supplements that have been okayed by our doctor. If you haven't already, start building your immune system now so it can help you in your fight against cancer.

God, my immune system is weak. Help me as I repair and strengthen my immunity. Help me establish good eating and lifestyle habits that will aid my body in fighting this cancer. Give me wise counsel from those who understand how my immune system can help this fearfully and wonderfully made body of mine. I pray for a restoration of full strength in my body so it can resist the advance of my cancer. May each cancer cell fall under the attack of renewed immunity from my body.

LOOKING TO JESUS

*Looking to Jesus, the founder and perfecter of
our faith, who for the joy that was set before him
endured the cross, despising the shame, and is
seated at the right hand of the throne of God.*
HEBREWS 12:2

When trouble strikes, it's easy to see the mountain in front of us instead of turning our eyes to Jesus, "the founder and perfecter of our faith." We must remember that our strength is in Jesus. Let's look to him.

Jesus, you are the founder and perfecter of my faith. For me, you endured the cross, despised the shame, and are now seated at the right hand of the Father's throne. Thank you for your loving care for me. Thank you that you vowed to never leave or forsake me... even during my battle with cancer. So it's to you I look, Jesus. I keep my eyes trained on you as a puppy looks affectionately and expectantly to its master. As I continue my cancer journey, Jesus, may I always turn away from worrying about the cancer in my body, and instead turn my eyes upon you—knowing your eyes are always on me.

WAITING

They who wait for the LORD shall renew their strength; they shall mount up with wings like eagles; they shall run and not be weary; they shall walk and not faint.

ISAIAH 40:31

No one likes to wait. Waiting is hard. It's especially hard when you're waiting to come through the cancer tunnel, back into the light of healthy living again. But waiting *on the Lord* is different. We're strengthened as we wait for the Lord. We "mount up with wings like eagles." We run without becoming weary. We do not faint, even during adversity. Wait, then, on the Lord.

God, it's hard for me to wait. I want to know what's going to happen *now*. I want to know the result of every lab test *now*. I want to know I'm going to be okay *now*. For that reason, Lord, I ask you to help me learn to wait on you. Help me set my clock by your eternal timepiece, not by my own impatient heart. The truth is, I need you to renew my strength. I need wings like eagles. Oh, how I need to not be weary! I want to walk and walk and walk and not feel faint. O Lord, forgive my impatience. Help me to trust...and wait.

THE GOD WHO SEES

[Hagar] called the name of the LORD who spoke
to her, "You are a God of seeing," for she said,
"Truly here I have seen him who looks after me."

GENESIS 16:13

Hagar was utterly rejected, abandoned after Abram left her to Sarai's abuse. But during her subsequent flight, Hagar came to know *El Roi*, the Hebrew name of God that translates to "the God who sees." And so he does.

God sees *all*. He sees you now. He has numbered the hairs on your head (Matthew 10:30)—even if there are only a few due to the effects of chemotherapy. Can you trust *El Roi*, the God who sees? Yes, you can. If Hagar could trust him in her desperation, so can you.

O God, how foolish of me to ever forget that you are *El Roi*. You are *my El Roi*. You not only see me now, but you saw me before my diagnosis. You knew what was coming and were abundantly there for me on that day—even if I, like Hagar, was unaware. You will be "the God who sees" each day of my cancer journey. You see the outcome and will be with me through it all. Therefore, I can echo Hagar and say, "Truly here I have seen him who looks after me."

LISTEN TO GOOD ADVICE

The way of a fool is right in his own eyes,
but a wise man listens to advice.
PROVERBS 12:15

No sooner is the word out about our cancer, than we start to receive advice from well-meaning acquaintances. One talent we need to develop is learning to sort out the good advice from the not-so-helpful advice. Listen to what others say, but always consider the source. And when in doubt, have the advice confirmed by another trusted authority on your support team.

God, some of my friends are offering me advice. "Try this remedy." "Try that treatment." "Don't let them do this surgery." "Stay away from that drug." Maybe some of them are right...or maybe they're wrong. Help me, Lord, to listen only to wise advice. Close my ears to well-meaning but ill-informed sages—including those on the Internet—who are not walking in my shoes. Remind me to carefully consider advice only from well-informed people whom I can trust and whose advice is confirmed by others on my support team.

UNCERTAINTY

Trust in the LORD with all your heart,
and do not lean on your own understanding.
In all your ways acknowledge him,
and he will make straight your paths.

PROVERBS 3:5-6

The path of a person with cancer is sometimes rocky...sometimes leads uphill...and yet at other times, it can be like a walk on a warm, sandy beach. Yet the end of the path itself is uncertain. Will we survive, or is this cancer God's way of ushering us into heaven? In either case, we need not fear. If we are acknowledging him in *all* our ways—even in our cancer—then he will make our path to health or to heaven straight.

God, thank you for my life. I love living, and I pray for many more years of serving you here on earth. With cancer, the doctors have no guarantees for how long I might live. I've known of cancer patients given a few months to live, who then went on for several more decades. Others were assured of remission, only to lose the battle within weeks. Lord, I'm here at your pleasure. I pray for more years, but I trust you with that decision. I pray most of all for a straight path.

In the Day of Trouble

Call upon me in the day of trouble;
I will deliver you, and you shall glorify me.
PSALM 50:15

A cancer diagnosis qualifies as a "day of trouble." Call on the Lord often during your cancer fight. He will deliver you. There's nothing selfish about praying for yourself. God often tells his people to call on him. He hears those prayers. Never be reluctant to cry out to God, to call on him in the day of trouble.

Father God, today I call upon you in my day of trouble. Hear my plea for help and healing as I fight cancer. According to your Word, deliver me—and I will in turn glorify you. Lord, reverse my adverse circumstances. Bring about restoration. Turn me away from this day of trouble, and bring me into days of blessing. But in all things, Lord, may you be glorified.

FEAR NOT

Fear not, for I am with you;
be not dismayed, for I am your God;
I will strengthen you, I will help you,
I will uphold you with my righteous right hand.

ISAIAH 41:10

Cancer can be a fearful thing—or not. We can choose to accept the fear that generally accompanies a cancer diagnosis, or we can engage in the battle with courage. Fear, though a natural emotion when we face cancer, changes nothing about our condition. So why entertain it? It's faith, not fear, that pleases God (Hebrews 11:6).

God, help me overcome the fear that crops up every so often as I think about my cancer diagnosis. Help me build my faith so I can stand against every fearful thought. When these thoughts first occur, remind me to cast them down immediately and replace them with thoughts of your love, protection, and healing.

Lord, I know that fear cannot change a thing about this dreaded disease. It only robs me of my joy and undermines my trust in you. May the only fear I choose to dwell on be the rightful fear of God—"the beginning of wisdom" (Psalm 111:10).

The Learning Curve

An intelligent heart acquires knowledge,
and the ear of the wise seeks knowledge.
Proverbs 18:15

When we're first diagnosed with cancer, we encounter a sharp learning curve. We find ourselves inundated with information about a topic we hoped we would never need to know about. But knowledge is power. It behooves us to be aware of our particular type of cancer and the available treatment options.

Father, it was not in my plan to have cancer. I never wanted to learn about malignant cells multiplying in my body and the ensuing effects. Help me, Lord, as I know I must learn what I can about my options. Bring the right, knowledgeable people my way. Help me tune in to conversations I'd rather tune out. Bring me not just correct information, but also the wisdom to apply what I learn. May my heart acquire the necessary knowledge, and may my ears listen to good advice.

MAKING DECISIONS

*I will instruct you and teach you in the way you
should go; I will counsel you with my eye upon you.*
PSALM 32:8

Being asked to make decisions about our treatment
and our future is yet another hard thing about
cancer. Surgery, chemo, or radiation? Are there other
treatment options? Should you participate in clinical
trials? Will a nutritionist help? If ever we needed God's
instruction on how to proceed, it's *now*. God's promise is to instruct and guide us, with his eye upon us.
Count on this.

Lord God, help. I have decisions to make about my
treatment, either now or in the near future. I can't
make these decisions alone. I need you to instruct and
teach me in the way I should go. Lord, keep your eyes
closely upon me. Counsel me with my ultimate good in
mind. Show me either through my doctors' advice, the
guidance of my support team, or in some other clear
way exactly what to do every step. And may I choose
the best options that will bring optimal results. Give
me perfect peace as I make the necessary decisions
about my future.

LAUGH WHEN YOU CAN

Our mouth was filled with laughter,
and our tongue with shouts of joy;
then they said among the nations,
"The LORD has done great things for them."

PSALM 126:2

It may be hard at first to laugh in the presence of cancer, but there is a release of joy we experience when we laugh at even our direst circumstances. And why can we laugh at such a time? Because we know that God is in control and has matters well in hand. The realization that our situation is in the hands of an almighty, sovereign, and omniscient God can remove the spirit of heaviness and exchange it for a cloak of joy.

Dear Lord, it seems hard to laugh at cancer, but in truth, cancer has no power that you cannot quell. You are greater than this disease. You can bring healing with a single touch of your hand. Yes, God, I can laugh today at this powerless malady called cancer. I can smile in the face of the severest trial because "the LORD has done great things" for me. Praise you, Lord, for heavenly humor in a hellish situation.

STRONG IN SPIRIT

Have I not commanded you? Be strong
and courageous. Do not be frightened,
and do not be dismayed, for the LORD your
God is with you wherever you go.
JOSHUA 1:9

Courage comes from the knowledge that God is with us during our cancer battle wherever we go—even into the lab, the chemo room, the operating room, and under the radiation rays. He's always there.

Lord, you actually command me to be strong and courageous during my cancer journey. You tell me not to be frightened or dismayed...and all because you are with me. Thank you, God, for your presence wherever I go. Thank you for being by my side throughout all my days. I praise you that you see ahead and assure me nothing is coming down the road that I can't handle with you beside me. When I lack strength and courage, Lord, lift me up. Help me stand strong. Today I worship you for the overcoming power you give me.

DON'T BE ANGRY

Refrain from anger, and forsake wrath!
Fret not yourself; it tends only to evil.
PSALM 37:8

Cancer angers us. It steals our health and, to some degree, our enjoyment of life. Yet uncontrolled anger does harm to our bodies and our spiritual life. As we continue our battle, let's set aside anger and the evil that comes with it, and instead pursue peace of mind.

Father, sometimes my cancer stirs up anger within me. I'm not even sure who or what I'm angry at. The cancer—yes, for sure. But that does no good. Cancer can't respond to the anger I direct toward it. Sometimes I get angry at myself if I haven't made healthy choices, but that, too, isn't helpful now. Lord, sometimes I'm even tempted to be angry at you for allowing this. But no matter where my anger is directed, Father, help me lay it aside. Help me as I forsake wrath. Grant me peace in place of anger.

Day by Day

*This is the day that the LORD has made;
let us rejoice and be glad in it.*
PSALM 118:24

How do we fight cancer? Day by day. We shouldn't look ahead and project fear into our future. Nor should we harbor regrets about a past we cannot change. What we ought to do is take today as a gift from God, enjoying it and praying that it brings us one day closer to restored health.

Thank you, Lord, for this day. Yes, *this* day. I rejoice in all you have for me, even as I deal with the cancer that tries to bring me down. Rather than let the cancer win, I will praise you for this day. I will "rejoice and be glad in it," if for no other reason than that you have created it for me. I receive this gift with thanksgiving and joy.

Lord, I try not to look ahead, but I do pray for the gift of many more days to rejoice in you. I give you praise for each one, taking none of them for granted.

The Wilderness

Behold, I am doing a new thing;
now it springs forth, do you not perceive it?
I will make a way in the wilderness
and rivers in the desert.

Isaiah 43:19

When we're walking through the desert experience we call "cancer," we need God to bring about a new thing. We need a river in our dry land and a way through the wilderness. And God promises just that.

Lord, it's dry in this cancerous desert. Please bring forth the rivers of hope that you're so good at creating. Let me find a small blessing—even a stream or spring—each new day, carving a way through my wilderness. Be my guide, my companion, my adviser, and my comforter on this journey. Bring new life to me, Lord. Remind me of the preciousness in all of life, including this day you've gifted to me. Open my eyes to witness your rivers in the desert. Praise you, Lord. Truly, I praise you!

Healthy Thinking

Beloved, I pray that all may go well
with you and that you may be in good
health, as it goes well with your soul.
3 John 2

The apostle John prayed that the recipient of his third epistle (Gaius) would be in good health, both physically and spiritually. May God allow that to be our verse as we move forward in our battle against cancer.

Lord, I love how John was concerned about Gaius's physical and spiritual health. I pray, likewise, for my own good health. First, of course, for the health of my soul. I pray for maturity, realizing this cancer may be a pathway leading to spiritual growth. I pray also for my body. I pray that you will continue to reverse the effects of cancer and bring me through this ordeal to restored health. Finally, I pray that "all may go well" with me. There is much on my plate these days, Lord, and I pray for your help in accomplishing all that must be done. Thank you for watching so lovingly over my soul—and my body.

Ask for the Best

You do not have, because you do not ask.
James 4:2

Asking for healing may seem presumptuous, but we know that God does heal. He's the same yesterday, today, and forever (Hebrews 13:8)—and we know from today's verse that we don't have because we don't ask. So let's ask.

Lord, cancer is hard on me. I could wish it away, but wishing does no good. The oncologist is doing what can be done medically, and I'm thankful for that. But in the Bible, you are revealed as the great healer. Father, giver of perfect gifts, I ask for healing. Place your restoring hand on my body and bring about the destruction of the cancer within. I ask with faith and leave it to you. Thank you, Lord, for your healing power.

Church Support

*Beloved, let us love one another, for love
is from God, and whoever loves has
been born of God and knows God.*
1 John 4:7

During stressful times—such as a financial crisis, a broken relationship, or, in our case, a cancer diagnosis—it's vital to have a good support group from our church or Bible study, in addition to our cancer support team.

Don't be shy about asking for help from your church when you need it. Christianity majors in loving and caring for one another. Give others the opportunity to minister to you in whatever way they can. Yes, it takes humility. But please make your needs known if they're not known now. If you have no church affiliation, ask to speak to a hospital chaplain, or ask one of your support team members for a recommendation.

Lord, part of the battle I'm facing includes loneliness and the need for practical assistance from others. I pray you'll give me the courage to ask for help as I need it. May my requests fall on receptive ears. I know people are busy, but you can put it on the hearts of my spiritual community to be attentive to my needs. Help me to avail myself of their help, with the understanding that I need to do for myself those things I can do. Lord, if there are helpers who might come to my aid whom I'm unaware of, I pray you'll guide me in connecting with them. And God, as my health improves, may I remember what it's like to need help and offer myself to the aid of others in their trials.

Don't Withdraw from Life

I lie awake; I am like a lonely
sparrow on the housetop.
Psalm 102:7

Even though we realize others have gone through the cancer experience—and even now, others are on the same road we're on—we often can't help feeling alone. Along with that, we can sometimes be tempted to withdraw from life itself. But we mustn't. We must live boldly, even in this difficult time. Live on and trust fully in God.

Lord, sometimes I feel alone in my cancer fight. Yes, I know others have walked this path, and I know others are now in the same place I am. We really are like a nation to ourselves. But God, help me to stay fully engaged in the arena of life. Please encourage me so I don't withdraw from life or become like the "lonely sparrow on the housetop," lying awake...worrying, wondering, and counting all the things that might happen, while knowing full well they also might not happen. Help me keep a positive outlook in the days ahead. Awaken me to opportunities for reaching out and being a part of this wonderful life you've given me. Thank you, Lord, for loving me.

Job's Latter Half

*The LORD blessed the latter days of
Job more than his beginning.*
Job 42:16

Yes, Job had it rough. His "cancer"—that is, his accumulated hardships—was quite malignant. He lost it all, except for his wife and his life. But after he encountered God in his misery, what happened? The latter portion of his life exceeded his earlier days. May it be so with us as well.

God, I long for the days when I can live out the rest of my life enjoying the blessings you have planned for me. Like Job, I've been full of questions, heard counsel from both wise and unwise friends, and suffered loss. Yet I'm sure Job would have said it was all worth going through to get to the final part of life that was rich with your blessings. Lord, I pray that for myself. I pray for a future filled with your plans and purposes for me. Like Job, may I declare, "I had heard of you by the hearing of the ear, but now my eye sees you" (Job 42:5).

Cancer Is Just a Detour

Blessed is the man who remains steadfast
under trial, for when he has stood the test
he will receive the crown of life, which God
has promised to those who love him.
James 1:12

God willing, cancer has come to pass, but not to stay. Hopefully, this road of bumps and gullies is simply a detour that will take us where we really want to be...after we steadfastly endure the trial. The crown awaiting us will be worth it all.

Father, I want to be a "blessed" person. I see from your Word that blessing comes from remaining "steadfast under trial," and that a crown of life awaits me at the end of the trial. Lord, steady my ship and help me remain devoted to you in the rough waters of cancer. As I scan the horizon, give me faith to see the calm waters ahead. This present tempest is but a passing storm, one I can surely ride out with the wind of your spirit at my back. Grant me that breeze, Lord—that warm, comforting breeze sending me closer to the calm waters ahead.

TREAT YOURSELF

For no one ever hated his own flesh,
but nourishes and cherishes it, just as Christ does
the church, because we are members of his body.
EPHESIANS 5:29-30

When our body hurts, it's amazing what even a small treat can do: a favorite meal, a walk on the beach or in the woods, a full-body massage. These and more can temporarily alleviate any pain we're suffering—even if the pain is in our emotions, not our body.

Don't hate your flesh. Nourish and cherish it during the rough times.

Dear Father, thank you for the small pleasures that relieve my pain. The release of endorphins is surely part of your design of my body for just such a time as this. As I continue on this unwanted journey, I pray for more of these little treats I can give my suffering body—especially on those days when I'm recovering from a chemo or radiation session. Lord, lead me to the most efficient ways to let my body know I care for it in its pain.

THE LONG VIEW

For I know the plans I have for you, declares
the LORD, plans for welfare and not for
evil, to give you a future and a hope.
JEREMIAH 29:11

Fear can paralyze us. We can become afraid when all we imagine is a bleak future of chemo, radiation, or surgery—none of which is a guarantee of remission. Instead of fearing, though, let's use our faith to imagine a brighter future...one with hope.

Lord, thank you that you have my time in your hands. The sand will not run out of my hourglass until you say so. I pray for each day, month, year, and even decade that you may have ahead for me. As I move forward with my treatment, I will keep my eyes on you as the master of my life. I look to you to keep the sand pouring through the hourglass. Thank you for your plans of welfare...and of a future and hope.

YOUR FELLOW TRAVELERS

Let all that you do be done in love.
1 CORINTHIANS 16:14

We're never alone as we battle cancer. We're on a road with many fellow travelers. While it's normal to focus on our own fight, it's good to remember our fellow combatants. Do you know someone on the same battlefield? Pray for them. Encourage them. Let them know they're loved by God—and by you.

Father, we are a large army fighting cancer. Help us prevail over our cancerous enemy. I pray for those I know who are having a tough time of it right now. Ease their pain, give them hope, and help me encourage them to stand strong and not give up. I pray for their support team of medical professionals and for their families. Give them wisdom and wise counsel as they support their loved one. Lord, keep us in your love, always

Giants in the Land

*Then Caleb quieted the people before Moses,
and said, "Let us go up at once and take
possession, for we are well able to overcome it."
But the men who had gone up with him
said, "We are not able to go up against the
people, for they are stronger than we."*

Numbers 13:30-31 nkjv

Most of the spies sent out to investigate Canaan came back with a bad report. The land was lush and beautiful...but it was filled with giants. The fearful spies wanted to give up God's promised land, fearing the worst. But Caleb and Joshua believed God. Sure, there were giants in the land, but they could be defeated.

We are up against a giant we call "cancer." But, like Caleb and Joshua, we must face this giant with courage and not cower in fear at our diagnosis. We must be strong.

O God, there are giants in the land! The giant of cancer threatens to devour me. Help me, Lord, by giving me faith like Caleb and Joshua. Empower me to stay the course and come out the other side of the fight into the land of health and prosperity. God, unless you are my strength, I will surely faint in the presence of the giants. Remind me daily, Lord, of *your* power to bring victory.

You Are Not Your Cancer

*You are a chosen race, a royal priesthood, a holy
nation, a people for his own possession, that you
may proclaim the excellencies of him who called
you out of darkness into his marvelous light.*

1 Peter 2:9

Sometimes we Christians have an identity crisis. We assume the identity the world puts on us and forget the true identity God gives us as his children. We may look in the mirror and see an unfamiliar face as cancer or our treatments make changes in our appearance. But our God-given identity trumps the mirror and trumps our feelings. *We are not our cancer.* We are not victims. We are a royal race. We are a holy nation...a people for God's own possession. Let's proclaim his excellencies and our glorious identity.

Father God, I thank you that you have created me as I am. I thank you that I'm your child, your own possession, part of a chosen race of people called out of darkness into your marvelous light. When I forget who I am, when I assume the identity of a victim and not a victor, remind me of my true identity—an *overcoming* identity.

LEARNING TO LOVE

Love is patient and kind; love does not envy or
boast; it is not arrogant or rude. It does not insist
on its own way; it is not irritable or resentful;
it does not rejoice at wrongdoing, but rejoices with
the truth. Love bears all things, believes all things,
hopes all things, endures all things. Love never ends.
1 CORINTHIANS 13:4-8

One of the few upsides of cancer is that we are faced with our utter dependence on God. We are forced to trust him with our future. Another upside is that cancer can teach us to love more effectively. Cancer diminishes a lot of the daily props that normally keep us occupied: our jobs, homelife, hobbies, sports, current events. They all pale when we battle cancer. As those things lessen in importance, we can see love is all that really matters.

God, you are the perfect example of love. You give without reservation. You are patient and kind, never arrogant or rude. You rejoice in truth. Your love never ends. Help me, Lord, as I look to the ones in my life you've called me to love. May I truly bear all things. May I believe in them, hope for them, and endure for them. May my love, like yours, never end.

Pray for Researchers

It is the glory of God to conceal things,
but the glory of kings is to search things out.
Proverbs 25:2

Hopefully someday there will be a cure for all cancers. Those cures just haven't been fully discovered yet. Advances have been made, and many cancers are curable or at least treatable. Every day researchers are looking for those elusive cures. It's their calling to "search things out."

In the meantime, we who are part of the cancer community can support these researchers with our prayers. We can also financially support credible organizations that are at the forefront of fighting cancer. In praying for them, we're also praying for ourselves.

Dear Lord, I pray for those who are on the front lines of researching cures for cancer. Give them wisdom beyond themselves. Awaken curiosity to try even the most unlikely treatments. Raise up a new generation of eager, inquisitive minds who won't stop experimenting until a cure is found. I pray, too, for those who are involved in clinical trials. May much be gained through their volunteered efforts. Lord, bring forth the knowledge that will end cancer forever.

CELEBRATIONS ALONG THE WAY

Praise the LORD!
Praise God in his sanctuary;
praise him in his mighty heavens!
Praise him for his mighty deeds;
praise him according to his excellent greatness!
PSALM 150:1-2

Sometimes when we meet with the oncologist, we can almost read the news on his or her face. Good news, praise the Lord! Not-so-good news...well, it's hard to praise God, but he is still God no matter what the lab tests say. When the news *is* good, it calls for a celebration. But whether the news is good or bad, there is always reason to give God thanksgiving and praise. And thanksgiving and praise can have their own positive effect on our return to health.

God, I praise you today. You are worthy of all honor, glory, and worship. Good news or bad, I exalt you. I praise you with my lips for your mighty deeds and excellent greatness. With all that is within me, I worship you and I trust you. I celebrate you in my life and acknowledge you as the Lord of my body, soul, and spirit. Praise you, Father!

GOD IS SOVEREIGN

Many are the plans in the mind of a man,
but it is the purpose of the LORD that will stand.
PROVERBS 19:21

Trusting in God's sovereignty is a great comfort as we endure cancer. We know by faith that God's plans for our life will *always* prevail. And we know that prayer can move his hand. In his sovereignty, we find complete rest.

Father, I trust in you as my sovereign God. You are never surprised or undone by the events that transpire in my life. You never say, "Wow, I didn't see that coming!" My very cancer was no shock to you. You have always had my life in your hands, as you do this very day. I can trust my future to your sovereignty. I can pray with the assurance that you are able to fulfill your every plan for me. Your purpose for me will stand. Nothing will be lost. No cancer, no accident, no hand of man can thwart your plan for me. For this and so much more, I am thankful.

The Joy of the Lord

The joy of the LORD is your strength.
NEHEMIAH 8:10

When we are weak, we need strength. Yet we often neglect to look for our strength in the joy of the Lord. Knowledge of God brings joy. Loving God brings joy. Sitting in his presence brings joy. When our strength is weak, may we turn to the Lord and receive his rejuvenating joy.

Lord, I praise you for the joy you give me—the joy that makes me strong in the days of my weakness. May my need for strength remind me to turn to you and simply sit in your presence, basking in your joy. Lord, increase my ability to enjoy you and rejoice in you. Expand my capacity to know your joy.

You're Not Finished

The LORD will fulfill his purpose for me;
your steadfast love, O LORD, endures forever.
Do not forsake the work of your hands.
PSALM 138:8

When cancer strikes, we're tempted to think God has forgotten us. But God sees our every circumstance. He knows how to cause our days of cancer to eventually work for our good and to become a part of fulfilling his purpose for us (Romans 8:28). This happens by faith. We trust God to bring about his divine purpose for all that happens in our life, including cancer. No, he has not forsaken us and will not forsake us. *Ever.*

Father, I thank you that as your child you have a prepared purpose for my life—a purpose you will fulfill in due time. I trust that your steadfast love will see me through my hard days. I believe your Word that says you will not forsake the work of your hands. You will not forsake *me.*

Overcoming the Evil One

The thief comes only to steal and kill
and destroy. I came that they may
have life and have it abundantly.

John 10:10

The life of a believer in Christ is an abundant life. There is no lack for those who trust God. However, our adversary, Satan, has his own plan for our lives. That plan is one of destruction. As we endure cancer, we must look to God for his abundance as we also resist the efforts of the enemy to destroy us. We must overcome every satanic attack through prayer and the intercession of our support team. Pray for the abundant life God has for you.

Thank you, Lord, for the abundant life you've promised me. I pray that every drop of abundance you have for me will not go unlived by me. I pray against the powers of darkness that would rob me of your abundance. I resist Satan's power to steal, kill, and destroy. Lord, I overcome the enemy's strategies to bring me down by turning to you. I rejoice in you and cast down every evil thought or imagination that Satan suggests to me. Lord, in you I claim total victory over Satan and his minions.

Be Filled

Be filled with the Spirit.
EPHESIANS 5:18

It's always timely to ask, "Who is filling us?" Are we filled with ourselves and all the self-oriented desires of the natural man? Or are we filled with joy and the Holy Spirit? Have we heeded God's command to "be filled with the Spirit"? Therein is victory assured.

Lord, fill me with your Holy Spirit. May I overflow with the joy that is the fruit of your Spirit. May *every* fruit of the Spirit be seen in me. And God, as I prayerfully consider my treatment options, may the Holy Spirit within me guide me in making the right choices. May the abiding Spirit work in my body for healing and restoration. Lord, by faith, I do receive your Holy Spirit in my life.

HE IS LORD

God has highly exalted him and bestowed on
him the name that is above every name, so
that at the name of Jesus every knee should
bow, in heaven and on earth and under the
earth, and every tongue confess that Jesus
Christ is Lord, to the glory of God the Father.
PHILIPPIANS 2:9-11

Jesus is Lord. Jesus is *your* Lord. Proclaim him so today. Know that he is Lord of your body, soul, and spirit. He is the Lord who keeps you for himself (Psalm 121:3). You can trust him fully.

Dear God, I confess that Jesus Christ *is* Lord, to the glory of you, my heavenly Father. I confess that Jesus is Lord over *all* my life—Lord over my body and Lord over my soul. I give my body and its health over to Jesus. May he mend its broken places, heal my infirmities, and restore my health. To you, O Lord, I give all the praise and glory.

THE PROMISES OF GOD

His divine power has granted to us all things
that pertain to life and godliness, through the
knowledge of him who called us to his own glory
and excellence, by which he has granted to us his
precious and very great promises, so that through
them you may become partakers of the divine
nature, having escaped from the corruption
that is in the world because of sinful desire.
2 PETER 1:3-4

Those live best who live by the promises of God. It's through God's promises that Peter says we "become partakers of the divine nature" and escape the corruption in the world due to sinful desires. All of a Christian's life should be built on the promises of God revealed in the Bible—promises of peace, joy, love, and eternal life to all who believe. Lean hard on God's promises in the Bible as you battle cancer.

God, I thank you for your precious promises. Help me build my life around your every provision for me. Guide me as I apply the promises in your Word to my health and the hope of overcoming the cancer that has invaded my body. As I read your Word, I pray your Holy Spirit would highlight the promises I need to sustain me. May those verses stir my heart the moment I read them. As I commit your promises to memory, I pray they would come to mind in every needed circumstance. Bring your Word and your promises to pass in my life, Lord.

You Are Unique

O LORD, you have searched me and known me!
You know when I sit down and when I rise up;
you discern my thoughts from afar.
You search out my path and my lying down
and are acquainted with all my ways.
PSALM 139:1-3

We serve a God acquainted with all our ways. There is nothing about us God is not concerned with or does not know. He is aware of our every thought and worry. He has fashioned each of us uniquely to be his own possession. He cares for us with a love we cannot fully comprehend this side of eternity.

Wow, God! I'm always amazed when I think of how you created me as a unique person, different from everyone else, with various talents and abilities. You know everything about me. There's nothing I can hide from you. Lord, you know about the cancer I'm battling. You know how I'm struggling with a temptation to worry. And yet, because you are my creator and the fashioner of my body, I know I can trust you to deal with this cancer as you desire. Lord, thank you for the unique plan you have for my life. Thank you for being "acquainted with all my ways."

GRACE AND MERCY WILL
SEE YOU THROUGH

*Let us then with confidence draw near to the
throne of grace, that we may receive mercy
and find grace to help in time of need.*
HEBREWS 4:16

Do we ever hesitate to draw near to God's throne
of grace? We shouldn't. God invites us to come to
him with all our burdens and concerns, especially in
our time of need.

Draw near, my friend. God is there to listen.

Father, at your invitation, I draw near to your throne
of grace with confidence. Not only confidence that you
hear, but confidence that you care about me and will
send mercy and grace to see me through my present
ordeal. I pray boldly for your intervention in every part
of my life. My health, my family, my weaknesses, my
finances—every part of me, Lord, I bring to your throne
of grace. See me through.

COUNTING ON A MIRACLE

*His name—by faith in his name—has made
this man strong whom you see and know, and
the faith that is through Jesus has given the man
this perfect health in the presence of you all.*

ACTS 3:16

As believers in Christ, we know that miracles still happen. In the blink of an eye our cancer can be gone. Or a slower miracle might happen as we're healed through natural means or through a chemo cocktail, radiation, or the hands of a surgeon. However it happens, healing is a miracle—one we should pray for. We can't be shy about wanting restored health. God does not resent our prayers for healing. But we must ask in faith, trusting his will.

God, you have always been able to heal miraculously or through the agency of natural means or medicine. Whatever way you may choose, I do pray boldly for that miracle in my fight against cancer. Help me, Lord. Help me when my faith is weak, but still alive. Help me in the face of adversity. Lord, may the healing power in the name of Jesus be active in my life. To you alone I give the praise for restored health.

Don't Underestimate God

For nothing will be impossible with God.
Luke 1:37

When we're dealing with cancer, we're often tempted to think the worst. Our faith takes a back seat to the gathering black clouds of depression. At such times, it's imperative that we push away those black clouds and put our faith back where it belongs—on the front lines of our battle. We serve a God for whom *nothing is impossible.* Never forget that.

Lord, I believe that with you, nothing is impossible. You are the God who still creates miracles. You still mend the broken and heal the sick. Father, I present myself to you as one who needs your restoring touch. I pray for renewed health that only you can grant, even if it comes through the hands of my doctors. I pray for stamina, divine strength, and most of all, the will to be made whole again. Lord, show yourself as the one for whom nothing is impossible.

GOD'S WORD IS YOUR LAMP

Your word is a lamp to my feet
and a light to my path.
PSALM 119:105

When we're walking in the dark, we need light on our path. As we travel through cancer, we desperately need God's lamp in order to see clearly what's ahead.

God, your Word is my lamp throughout this cancer experience. Light my path by showing me how to respond with faith to every new twist in the road. May you provide more and more light each day through the faithful promises and comforting psalms in your Word. Set up guardrails along the way so I remain firmly on the path on which your light shines. Keep me from veering off onto dark detours that end in confusion. O Lord, light my way!

REST

Come to me, all who labor and are heavy laden,
and I will give you rest. Take my yoke upon you,
and learn from me, for I am gentle and lowly
in heart, and you will find rest for your souls.
For my yoke is easy, and my burden is light.
MATTHEW 11:28-30

Cancer often causes us to be "heavy laden." But one of God's greatest gifts for the weary is *rest*. Since the burden of cancer is not light, we must take the Lord's burden on ourselves and give him ours. Then we will find rest for our souls. That's a promise.

Dear Father, thank you for rest when I'm worn out from tests, doctors' appointments, treatments, follow-ups, trips to the pharmacy...and, not least of all, bone-tired exhaustion from battling cancer. Thank you that when I find rest in you, I also find a source of renewed strength. Today, Lord, I just want to lean hard on you and release my worry. I will take on your easy yoke and light burden. O Lord, how gentle they are!

GOD, THE GIVER OF GOOD GIFTS

*Every good gift and every perfect gift is from above,
coming down from the Father of lights, with whom
there is no variation or shadow due to change.*
JAMES 1:17

God never changes. He is always good and is always the giver of perfect gifts. Look to him for every gift you need. He will provide.

Lord, thank you for your kindness as demonstrated by the gifts you've given to me. I praise you that you never change. Truly there is no variation or shadow with you—only light.

Father, you see my present need. I pray for the gift of restored health. I pray for daily strength and motivation to run the course set before me. I honor you for your giving nature and for the full attention you give me daily. With you as my provider, I have no reason to worry. Help me look for your perfect gifts every day—even the small, but still appreciated gifts such as a hot cup of coffee, a funny joke, a child's laugh, and a tasty meal. Lord, I receive them all with gratitude.

A Difficult Road

It is the Lord who goes before you.
He will be with you; he will not leave you or
forsake you. Do not fear or be dismayed.
Deuteronomy 31:8

If we wonder what's wrong with us for being concerned or worried about our health, we need wonder no longer—we're simply normal. It's natural to be concerned when cancer or other ailments assail us. God knows we have those feelings, and that's why he so often comforts us with reassurances of his presence throughout our ordeal. It's good news that he not only goes before us, but that he is also with us and will not forsake us. Thus, we have no reason to fear or be dismayed.

Lord, cancer is not something I would ever choose for myself or even for my worst enemy. And yet here I am, walking the cancer road, unsure of where it leads. I can only thank you that I never have been alone on this road. You have been with me all along, even when I've been unaware of your presence beside me. Thank you for your promise never to forsake me. Lord, I trust in you and will not fear or be dismayed as I continue along this difficult road.

Mustard-Seed Faith

Truly, I say to you, if you have faith like a
grain of mustard seed, you will say to this
mountain, "Move from here to there," and it will
move, and nothing will be impossible for you.
MATTHEW 17:20

Must we have great faith to experience the Lord's work within us as we move through the cancer process? No, not at all. We need only have faith the size of a small mustard seed to move the cancer mountain. Our small faith is in a very large God. He can blast a pass through the mountain...or remove it entirely. Nothing is impossible if we have mustard-seed faith.

God, you see my teaspoon of faith. I believe—but help my unbelief (Mark 9:24). Help me increase my measure of faith so as to move this cancerous mountain in my life. Lord, nothing is impossible with you. So I pray that my faith, small as it is, will sustain me throughout my cancer journey. And may my mustard-seed faith be something I can share with others along the way. Lord, send me a cancer comrade for whom I can pray and to whom I can share my small faith in a great God.

Perfect Peace

You keep him in perfect peace
whose mind is stayed on you,
because he trusts in you.
Isaiah 26:3

We can have peace throughout our cancer journey...and not just an ordinary peace. The promise is for *perfect* peace as we keep our mind stayed on him, not on our cancer.

Father, my mind often drifts back to the cancer in my body. But I know I should keep my mind stayed on you, instead of allowing cancer to be my focus. As I trust in you, help me to keep my mind—and my eyes—focused on you. When I think of my cancer, remind me to turn my head away and adjust my gaze to you. Lord, perfect peace throughout the journey is my prayer.

Reigning in Life

If, because of one man's trespass, death
reigned through that one man, much more
will those who receive the abundance of
grace and the free gift of righteousness reign
in life through the one man Jesus Christ.
Romans 5:17

Cancer can quickly shove us under a pile of worry, fear, and what-ifs. We can't let that happen. We're called to reign in life. That means being above our circumstances, not below them.

God, thank you for your abundance of grace, even in the face of a serious disease. Thank you for the free gift of righteousness that allows me to reign in life—to reign over cancer and every adversity that comes my way. Thank you that because of Jesus, I can be on top of the pile of circumstances I face. I can reign over all my troubles. Praise you, Father.

Praise as Medicine

With my mouth I will give great thanks to the
Lord; I will praise him in the midst of the throng.
PSALM 109:30

Praise can bring about change. It can change us, and, in some measure, it can change our circumstances. Praise, in fact, can improve our health as we turn away from the worry and negativity that bring us down, and instead turn our face upward to God in praise.

Why not praise him out loud today? Vocalize your worship to God.

Lord, I praise you today. I sing hallelujah to your name; I worship you as my God. In you I glory, Lord. I turn my heart fully toward you. In praise, I reject all the worry and fear attached to me. In praise, I accept the good gift of health and healing you may bring my way. May I never let a day go by without offering my sacrifice of praise.

THE POWER OF SURRENDER

*I appeal to you therefore, brothers, by the
mercies of God, to present your bodies as
a living sacrifice, holy and acceptable to
God, which is your spiritual worship.*

ROMANS 12:1

To surrender is to give up control. Paul admonishes
the Roman Christians to present their bodies as a living sacrifice to God. How much more should we who
experience the cancer journey surrender our bodies to
God, our creator?

Father God, here is my body. You created it in my
mother's womb. You have watched over me through
the years, even when I was unaware of your presence.
Now my body has been attacked by cancer, and you
are the one with the power to determine the result of
this attack. Lord, I offer a prayer of total surrender. Use
me for your purposes. My body is yours; may it be holy
and acceptable to you.

An Awareness of Heaven

*To me to live is Christ, and to die is gain. If I am
to live in the flesh, that means fruitful labor for
me. Yet which I shall choose I cannot tell. I am
hard pressed between the two. My desire is to
depart and be with Christ, for that is far better.*
Philippians 1:21-23

A cancer diagnosis is not the end of the world. Far
from it. So many advances have been made that
many people diagnosed with cancer continue to live
full and productive lives for years after their diagnosis.

However, some do not. Eventually, some who are
diagnosed will die. But for the Christian, it really is a
win-win situation. Paul himself was undecided whether
he preferred to remain in his earthly body or to be
present with the Lord. One day—from whatever the
cause—we shall be in that glorious place where there
is no more pain, no more crying, no more death...and
no more cancer.

Lord, as I pray for an extension of my earthly life, I also
want to become aware of my heavenly home, prepared and waiting for me. May I sense the glories of
heaven while here on earth. As I look heavenward, I
pray you'll increase my longing to be with you and see
you face to face.

GROWING GOOD FRUIT

By this my Father is glorified, that you bear
much fruit and so prove to be my disciples.
JOHN 15:8

We must not waste our cancer days. God has fruit he wants to produce in us as we endure through our cancer. In bearing fruit, even in harsh conditions, we prove to be his disciples.

Lord Jesus, without you I can bear no fruit. But if you will plant seeds in my heart and water them with hope as I battle cancer, surely I will bear the fruit you desire.

Father, I pray you will be glorified in my life in some manner—perhaps currently unknown to me—as I bring forth good fruit that can be shared with others. Live through me by the power of your Holy Spirit. Do not let this cancer season of my life go to waste.

Giving Glory to God

So, whether you eat or drink, or whatever you do,
do all to the glory of God.

1 Corinthians 10:31

We are to do *all* to the glory of God. That includes bearing up through our cancer walk to the glory of God. By faith—and only by faith—can we imagine how God will receive glory from our ordeal.

God, facing cancer is hard. It's not what I expected at this time of my life, and yet here I am. All I can possibly do now is ask you to bring glory to yourself as I submit to you. I pray that through it all—the tests, the treatments, the prescriptions—you will be glorified. Remind me on my hardest days that, yes, even in *this* I can glorify God. May it be so, Lord.

A Grateful Heart

I give you thanks, O LORD, with my whole heart;
before the gods I sing your praise;
I bow down toward your holy temple
and give thanks to your name for your
steadfast love and your faithfulness,
for you have exalted above all things
your name and your word.

PSALM 138:1-2

It takes faith to remain grateful when serious illness strikes. But we can do this. We can give thanks to God with our *whole* heart. Remember his steadfast love and his faithfulness. Yes, even now he remains faithful to you. His hand, sometimes hidden, is upholding you as you read and pray.

Lord, may your name and your Word be exalted above all things. Father, like David, "I bow down toward your holy temple and give thanks to your name for your steadfast love and your faithfulness." Lord, I sing your praise today. I glorify you with my whole heart—a heart that is truly grateful amid the turmoil of cancer.

BE CONFIDENT OF GOD'S WORK IN YOU

*He who began a good work in you will bring
it to completion at the day of Jesus Christ.*

PHILIPPIANS 1:6

God is *always* at work in the life of a believer. We can easily forget that, though, when trouble enters our life. But the truth is that cancer does not inhibit God's work in us. Many times cancer becomes a tool God can use for our ultimate good. But we will only see that through the eyes of faith. Even if our faith is weak, we still must be confident of what God is doing.

God, I believe you are at work in my life as I battle cancer. This dreaded disease is not a barrier for your determined work in me. I trust you to use this cancer in whatever way you desire to enhance the "good work" you're bringing to completion in my life. May your hand of blessing guide me in every decision I make. May your heart of compassion comfort me during my most painful days. May the end result of my cancer be to your glory.

Hidden with Christ

You have died, and your life is
hidden with Christ in God.
Colossians 3:3

There are some days we just want to run and hide. Hide from the doctor, hide from the chemo nurse, and even hide from our own family. At such times, we can escape to the place where our life is hidden with Christ. Safety and security await us there. God is our spiritual rest, and seeking times of quiet with him can be strengthening. Feel free to withdraw with Christ when you need rest.

O Lord, thank you for placing me in Christ. Thank you that my life is hidden with you, safe and secure. I praise you that my old life with all its sins and temptations has died. Now my life is anchored in Christ, my true hiding place.

Lord, when my body is tired and needs rest, I pray people will understand and give me time to be alone without distraction. Please grant me rest for both my spirit and my body.

WALKING ON WATER

Peter answered him, "Lord, if it is you, command
me to come to you on the water." He said, "Come."
So Peter got out of the boat and walked on the
water and came to Jesus. But when he saw the
wind, he was afraid, and beginning to sink he
cried out, "Lord, save me." Jesus immediately
reached out his hand and took hold of him, saying
to him, "O you of little faith, why did you doubt?"
And when they got into the boat, the wind ceased.
MATTHEW 14:28-32

For those of us with cancer, moving forward is like walking on water. The wind rages, and we fear we'll sink. And we *will* sink if our eyes remain on the stormy waves. But we must remember, as songwriter Helen Howarth Lemmel penned in her classic hymn, "Turn your eyes upon Jesus, look full in His wonderful face." All else "will grow strangely dim"…including cancer.

God, cancer is like raging waters splashing against the boat of my life. You bid me come to you by walking on these cancerous waters. Lord, I come. I keep my eyes on you—not on the raging waters of disease. When I foolishly glance at the turbulent waves and I begin to doubt, take hold of me. Cause the wind to cease. Comfort me.

"We Walk by Faith, Not by Sight"

We are always of good courage. We know that
while we are at home in the body we are away
from the Lord, for we walk by faith, not by sight.
2 Corinthians 5:6-7

All Christians must "walk by faith, not by sight." This becomes more apparent to us when we have cancer. It's now, more than ever, that we must be of "good courage."

Lord, I want to be "always of good courage." I want to "walk by faith, not by sight." Help me as I move ahead in what seems to be a dark cave of uncertainty. Help me know that you have set nothing in my path that will cause me to trip or fall as long as I trust you with every step I take. I know it's only while I'm here at home in my body that I must have faith and courage. Someday my faith will be complete when I'm present with you. Until then, may I be encouraged in the faith walk you've called me to make.

There is meaning in every journey
that is unknown to the traveler.
Dietrich Bonhoeffer

"In Quietness and Confidence"

*For thus says the Lord GOD, the Holy One of Israel:
"In returning and rest you shall be saved; in
quietness and confidence shall be your strength."*
ISAIAH 30:15 NKJV

God invites us to a time of "quietness and confidence." Here we will become strong. In rest, we can be saved. This is God's Word to us, so find rest today in the Lord—your advocate and your healer.

I praise you, Father, that I can return and have rest in you. Thank you that you provide strength in this place of "quietness and confidence." There is no storm here. No tumult. No raging seas or violent winds. All is calm in your presence. Peace is my portion today. Thank you, Lord, for being my rest station along the way, and for being my advocate and my healer.

WHEN YOU ARE WEAK

When I am weak, then I am strong.
2 CORINTHIANS 12:10

Cancer weakens our body and our spirits. So we need God's strength more than ever. We're compelled to trust him to see us through—and that's a good thing.

O Lord, this cancer weakens my body and my will. I don't have the strength or stamina that I used to have. I must rely on your strength to see me through, and surely your strength is enough. May your Holy Spirit within me empower me to do what I must do and remind me of the things I no longer need to do. Lord, your power raised Christ from the dead. May that same quickening spirit enliven my own body. Thank you for the weakness that exposes my need for your strength.

God's Hand Is Upon You

*Behold, I have engraved you on the palms of my
hands; your walls are continually before me.*
Isaiah 49:16

Through thick and thin, through health and disease,
through happiness and sadness, God's hand never
departs from us. He has engraved us on the palms of
his hands. We are his. Forever his.

God, thank you for engraving my life on the palms of
your hands. Thank you that there will never be a time
when you're not with me—strengthening me, encouraging me, reminding me of your love. I find rest, deep
rest, in the palm of your hand. I find courage in knowing
your hand is upon me. I find strength from your mighty
arm upholding me. Thank you, Father.

Unshakable Faith

Let us be grateful for receiving a kingdom
that cannot be shaken, and thus let us offer
to God acceptable worship, with reverence
and awe, for our God is a consuming fire.
HEBREWS 12:28-29

Cancer shakes us. We quake with fear of the unknown future. But God is already there. He is Lord of the future and assures us we have nothing to fear. For this, let us be grateful.

Lord God, I offer up worship to you today with reverence and awe. You are a God worthy of all praise—not just for what you do, but simply for who you are. Lord, you are indeed a "consuming fire." You have brought me into a "kingdom that cannot be shaken." I pray that as this cancer attempts to shake me in every direction, I will stand firm with unshakable faith in your work through my life. May your consuming fire burn away all anxiety and worry about the future...for you are there and have instructed me to not be afraid.

In *All* Circumstances

*Give thanks in all circumstances; for this is
the will of God in Christ Jesus for you.*
1 THESSALONIANS 5:18

Cancer is a hard circumstance in which to remain thankful. But thankfulness in the midst of adversity is God's command for us. And being thankful can become a sort of release as we give our worries to God.

Heavenly Father, you must have a purpose for this cancer. Even though it may come from the enemy himself, you can turn his diabolical plans to my good as I entrust my cancer and its treatment to you. Therefore, I can be thankful that this cancer, under your authority, can be used for my profit. Lord, thank you for the work this cancer will accomplish. Thank you, too, for a good ending when the desired work has been completed.

You're Not Alone

Just as I was with Moses, so I will be with you.
I will not leave you or forsake you.
Joshua 1:5

When we have cancer, we can feel like we're alone in our battle. It seems like no one else knows what we're going through. That's an understandable response, but it's wrong. Others *do* know and care. Joshua thought he was alone...but God was with him, just as he was with Moses, and just as he is with you this very minute.

God, when this cancer makes me feel so alone, be with me. Remind me of your presence. Knit in me a kinship with Joshua and Moses and all others who feel like they're going through trials alone. Comfort us all with your Holy Spirit. Encourage us with your joy. Bless us with wise counselors regarding our illnesses and hardships. Stay here, Lord. Stay.

SURE-FOOTED FAITH

The apostles said to the Lord, "Increase our faith!"
LUKE 17:5

No one gets through life without trials. But what are we to do when trials come? Do we just melt under the weight and hope for the best?

Trials, if handled rightly, expose our level of faith for the purpose of expanding our ability to trust. Do we have the sure-footed faith that will carry us through even serious trials? Or is our faith weak? If it's weak, we must remember that God can handle our meltdowns as we grow "from faith to faith" (Romans 1:17 NKJV). He hears us cry, "Increase our faith!"

Lord, I've always thought of myself as having faith. Now in this cancer trial, my true level of faith is being revealed. I pray that I won't let this experience pass without allowing it to expand my ability to trust. Father, arrange this ongoing cancer trial so as to be a faith builder, but also an encourager as you prove yourself to be my provider, my covering, and my shelter. Lord, be with me in my faith meltdowns. May I quickly recover as I place my faith in you, my sure-footed God.

"Be Anxious for Nothing"

*Be anxious for nothing, but in everything by prayer
and supplication, with thanksgiving, let your
requests be made known to God; and the peace
of God, which surpasses all understanding, will
guard your hearts and minds through Christ Jesus.*

Philippians 4:6-7 nkjv

What a promise! We can experience the peace of God, "which surpasses all understanding." This peace will guard our hearts and minds as we pass through the troubling cancer valley. Cast your every anxiety on the Lord (1 Peter 5:7). Partake of his peace. Let it wash over you.

Father, I cast *all* my anxieties on you. I lay my worries at your feet. I offer thanksgiving and praise to you, along with my requests for health and wholeness. Lord, I receive your peace that surpasses all understanding. May it bring me calmness of mind, clarity, and hope for the future. May your peace guard my heart and mind through Christ Jesus.

GOD SEES ALL

A man's ways are before the eyes of the LORD,
and he ponders all his paths.

PROVERBS 5:21

Nothing escapes God's eye. He sees all. He watches as we undergo tests and treatments. He ponders our every path. When we grieve, he grieves with us. When we rejoice, he's rejoicing too. Knowing this brings assurance and security.

God, there are times when I wish my ways were not before your eyes. There are paths I've walked I would not want you to ponder. But now there's *this*. Lord, for this stage of my life, I *do* want your eyes upon me. I do want you to ponder this cancer path I must take. Father, be my walking companion every step of the way. Let my ways be before your eyes; watch me closely each day. Protect, heal, mend, comfort, and love me. Thank you, my Lord.

Jars of Clay

*We have this treasure in jars of clay, to show
that the surpassing power belongs to God and
not to us. We are afflicted in every way, but not
crushed; perplexed, but not driven to despair.*
2 Corinthians 4:7-8

God knows even more than we do how we're made
of simple clay. And yet in our utter weakness as
malleable men and women, God's power can rest on us
as we pass through our afflictions. We are not crushed.
We are often perplexed, but we have no need to despair.

Father, I'm just made of clay, and very easily influenced
by my circumstances. But I'd prefer for your divine
hand to mold me through my cancer experience. Lord,
I pray for your power to rest on this body of clay as I
battle cancer. When I feel afflicted and perplexed, let
me not be driven to despair. Encourage me, Lord, with
your joy and your presence. Though my flesh be clay,
may my spirit be strong and vibrant.

GOD WILL DELIVER

Many are the afflictions of the righteous,
but the LORD delivers him out of them all.

PSALM 34:19

There is an end to our cancer—either healing or heaven (which is a form of healing in itself). Until that end, we can know that deliverance from the Lord will come eventually. God's power always outlasts our afflictions. Cancer never wins the battle.

Father, this affliction of cancer is among the worst events in my life. Please deliver me speedily from this disease, or enable me to use my time with my loved ones purposefully. Give my doctors wisdom and my support team the faith to see this through with me. Lord, your praise is on my lips, no matter how or when deliverance comes.

I trust in you, heavenly Father, to heal me one way or another.

GOD IS NOT SILENT

After the earthquake a fire,
but the LORD was not in the fire;
and after the fire a still small voice.
1 KINGS 19:12 NKJV

When we're dealing with cancer, we can easily become hard-of-hearing in a spiritual sense. We might even think God has gone silent. Is he with us? Does he hear our pleas? Why doesn't he answer?

Yes, he is here, just as he always has been. Listen for his still, small voice.

God, perhaps I'm so focused on my cancer that I don't recognize you're here with me in the midst of all this. I have a hard time hearing your clear voice speaking comfort to me, allaying my fears. Lord, help me have ears to hear you. Help me to quiet myself so I can listen more intently. Give me the ability to hear you in ways I may not expect—through other people; through small, meaningful gifts; through the kindness of caregivers.

Thank you for never being silent, but always speaking—even in that still, small voice I love.

More Fruit

I am the true vine, and my Father is the vinedresser.
Every branch in me that does not bear fruit he
takes away, and every branch that does bear
fruit he prunes, that it may bear more fruit.
John 15:1-2

We are branches in God's vineyard. Christ is the true vine. God, in overseeing his vineyard, looks for branches in the vine that need pruning. The cutting away of the dead stems is painful, but the end result is more fruit. That is what God is after when he prunes us. Let's ask God to allow our cancer to prune away all that hinders the good fruit.

Father, master of the vineyard, I understand the need for pruning. As part of your vineyard, I do want to be more fruitful. I want to be more fully connected to the true vine, the Lord Jesus. This cancer will surely be a pruning process for me. I pray that the shears will not cut too deeply; I pray for endurance through the pain. Most of all, I rejoice that there will be greater fruit ahead.

SLOW MIRACLES

Do not overlook this one fact, beloved, that
with the Lord one day is as a thousand
years, and a thousand years as one day.
2 PETER 3:8

We all want miracles in our lives. We want a quick fix. Sometimes God, in his graciousness, does work "fast" miracles. But sometimes he also works "slow" miracles. Can we trust him when the healing process is slow? Yes, we can.

Father God, I know time for you is different than time for me. What seems so slow here on earth passes quickly before your eyes. You take time in working out your divine plan.

Lord, my body needs a miracle. Even a slow miracle would be welcome. I pray you'll consider my situation, Father, and bring healing to my body. Slow or fast—I'll take either one.

Firmness of Spirit

Be watchful, stand firm in the
faith, act like men, be strong.
1 Corinthians 16:13

Enduring cancer isn't for cowards. It's a hard trek we all would prefer to avoid. One side effect of cancer is that we often feel our emotional knees grow weak as our faith wavers during the many tests, treatments, and appointments. In those times we need to remind ourselves to stand firm and face our fight with bravery, not cowardice. We *must* be strong.

God, I have faith in you. There are times, though, when I feel my knees grow weak under the weight of my diagnosis. Help me be watchful, my eyes open to your work, so I can stand firm and carry on my battle like a determined soldier. I pray for strength in all areas of my life—physical, spiritual, and emotional. Be Lord of *all* my life, Father.

Slow Down

Be still before the Lord and wait patiently for him.
PSALM 37:7

I t's hard to be still when our body is undergoing a battle. All the more so if we feel we have much left to do and our time is short. In such instances, there is strength to be found in an unlikely place: the inner room of stillness. There we can be silent before the Lord, praising him, worshiping him, waiting for him, and trusting him that all his plans for us will be accomplished before we exit this life.

Father, still my heart. Still my emotions. Still my fears. Lord, help me turn inward to you and forget for a while all the outward distractions that pull me away from you like a magnet. Give me rest in the stillness as I wait patiently for you. Lord, may I sense your holy presence near me. May I be overwhelmed by your love for me. Lord, help me to slow down and wait for you.

Managing Pain

The night racks my bones,
and the pain that gnaws me takes no rest.
Job 30:17

Job knew pain. And just like him, we often wonder *why* we must experience such trials, even as we trust God to the best of our ability. Although pain screams at us, we simply *have* to remember God is with us through every stab.

One thing we can do is compare our pain with the pain of crucifixion. Would we prefer to be nailed, hands and feet, to a cross? Yes, Job knew pain, but so did Jesus...and his suffering was for *us*. We have to believe that the Savior who bore our sin through the agony of the cross can also help us endure the pain that racks our bones and gnaws at us without rest.

Lord, sometimes the pain that accompanies cancer seems too great to bear. And the treatment sometimes feels worse than the cancer. When I try to remember that others, too, have borne such pain, it doesn't always seem to relieve my own misery. Help me look instead to the response of Jesus, "who for the joy that was set before him endured the cross" (Hebrews 12:2). I pray for that joy still ahead. Bring it soon, Lord.

GOD'S BLESSING

He will bless those who fear the LORD,
both the small and the great.
PSALM 115:13

The fear of the LORD is clean,
enduring forever.
PSALM 19:9

If cancer is our present lot in life, we need God's blessing as we go through this valley. God's blessing is akin to God's favor. And that favor is promised to those who fear him. Cancer has a way of reminding us to fear the Lord and the awesome power of his nature.

Lord, I do not like this cancer. But it does remind me that in sickness and in health, I need to rightly fear you. You are awesome and worthy of the kind of fear that cleanses the soul. The fear that endures forever. Lord, in fearing you, I ask for your blessing, which you have promised to both great and small. I certainly qualify as small...so God, bless me with your favor as I move through my cancer treatment.

LIFE IS STILL BEAUTIFUL

The Spirit of God has made me,
and the breath of the Almighty gives me life.
JOB 33:4

God has gifted us with this earthly life. He didn't have to create us...but, in love, he did. God not only gives life, he also sustains our life. What a blessing for us to enjoy!

Lord, thank you for my life. You have been—and still are—faithful to me each and every day. Your Spirit made me, and your breath gives me daily life. Father, I pray for this wonderful gift to continue until you call me home, whenever that may be. I pray that while I'm here, I will continue to honor you, bless you, worship you, and be grateful—for this life now, and for eternal life to come.

"They Turned to the Lord"

Peter... found a man named Aeneas, bedridden
for eight years, who was paralyzed. And Peter
said to him, "Aeneas, Jesus Christ heals you;
rise and make your bed." And immediately he
rose. And all the residents of Lydda and Sharon
saw him, and they turned to the Lord.

Acts 9:32-35

As we endure cancer and its treatments, people are watching us. How are we responding?

In the book of Acts, the residents of Lydda and Sharon witnessed a healing, and it prompted revival there as they turned to the Lord. It would be wonderful if a miraculous healing of cancer would cause those close to us to turn to the Lord. But miracle or no miracle, our response to cancer is a witness to God's faithfulness during adversity. We must pray for our family and friends as they observe our faith in action.

Lord, I have friends and family who need to turn to you. For them, I pray my cancer journey will be a witness as to how someone who hopes in you handles adversity. On my bad days, when I may not respond as well as I should, I pray for them to understand and still know my faith is what sustains me. (A miracle would certainly be welcome too, Lord!)

THE SHADOW OF GOD'S WINGS

Keep me as the apple of your eye;
hide me in the shadow of your wings.

PSALM 17:8

He will cover you with his pinions,
and under his wings you will find refuge;
his faithfulness is a shield and buckler.

PSALM 91:4

It is such a joy to see ourselves as the apple of God's eye, hidden in the shadow of his wings, with his feathers covering us. What refuge! In his faithfulness, we find a shield as we pass through every affliction that comes our way...including cancer.

O Lord, thank you for your protection. What security I find hidden in the shadow of your wings! Your faithfulness is my shield and buckler from the ravages of cancer. I'm humbled at the truth that you see me as the apple of your eye. Lord, stay close as I bury myself in the comfort of your wings. Praise you, Lord, praise you!

THE BATTLE IS THE LORD'S

*Thus says the LORD to you, "Do not be afraid and
do not be dismayed at this great horde,
for the battle is not yours but God's."*
2 CHRONICLES 20:15

When we battle cancer, we must do so in the
strength of the Lord. He is our mighty warrior
in the fight. He will lead the charge against the enemy.
We must not be dismayed at the appearance of cancer.
God has this.

God, how freeing to know that this battle is really yours,
not mine. You are ahead of me in the battle, subduing
the enemy with your power. You send unseen warriors
to fight on my behalf. Lord, because this is your battle,
I will not fear or be dismayed. I will watch as you go to
battle for me. I will savor the outcome. Thank you, Lord,
for victory!

Outward Changes

We do not lose heart. Though our outer self is wasting away, our inner self is being renewed day by day.

2 Corinthians 4:16

Everyone alive is wasting away to some degree. Our bodies are made of perishable flesh. However, our inner self can be renewed daily, no matter what's happening to our body. Keep your inner self strong, in spite of what may be changing in your outer flesh.

Lord, this cancer has brought about changes to my body. Some I can see; some I can't. Father, strengthen my inner life so I can have the right attitude about these changes to my outer self. Lord, renew me each day. May my spiritual life be strong enough to impact even my outer life, giving me hope. I also continue to pray for your healing Holy Spirit to work the necessary changes in my body that will help restore my health. May each cell in my body be positively affected by your life in me.

FIX YOUR HEART ON GOD

My heart is fixed, O God, my heart is fixed:
I will sing and give praise.
PSALM 57:7 KJV

Trouble always seems to steer our heart to a wobbly place of worry. But we must fix our heart on God and insist that it stay fixed throughout our cancer ordeal. We can do this by singing praises to God.

Lord, thank you for a voice with which to praise you. I worship you and fix my heart fully on you. In every aspect of my life, I choose to trust you and believe you work things out for my best. Lord, keep my eyes looking toward you in the face of adversity. Do not allow distractions, such as cancer, to move my fixed heart. Keep me focused on you, Lord.

God's Will

Father, if you are willing, remove this cup from me.
Nevertheless, not my will, but yours, be done.
LUKE 22:42

Jesus prayed for the cup of suffering awaiting him at the cross to be removed from him—but then he added a "nevertheless" that set his own desire beneath the Father's will. We must do the same. We ask for the cup of cancer to be removed...but more importantly, we ask for God's will to be done.

God, you know my desire. Like Jesus, I want this cup to pass from me. I want to be restored to health. I don't want to endure the cross of suffering we call "cancer." But, like Jesus, I pray for your will to be done in my life. I want my will to become your will, Father. May it be done in my life as you so determine. Either way, I honor and praise you today.

NOT BY MIGHT, NOT BY POWER

Not by might, nor by power, but by
my Spirit, says the LORD of hosts.
ZECHARIAH 4:6

Sometimes it's hard to turn the battle over to the Lord. But if we will trust him in all things, especially with this hardship of cancer, we can see his divine power at work. He is the Lord of hosts.

God, I'm tired...but I praise you that while my might and power are weak and ineffective, your Spirit is mighty and can accomplish whatever it wishes. Lord, may your Holy Spirit infuse my body with your glorious strength. Increase my reliance on you, Father. Remind me daily to turn over the next 24 hours to you and allow your Spirit to take on the battle.

THE BEAUTY OF THE LORD

One thing have I asked of the LORD,
that will I seek after:
that I may dwell in the house of the LORD
all the days of my life,
to gaze upon the beauty of the LORD
and to inquire in his temple.

PSALM 27:4

What are our goals in this life and the next? David had one request of God: to dwell in his presence, gazing upon his beauty and inquiring of him in his temple. Such should be enough for any of us.

O Lord, like David, I long to dwell in your house forever, to gaze upon your beauty and to ask you many, many things. Even as I live here on earth, let me feel a nearness to you and experience a refining of my life's goals. As David's longing was to dwell with you "all the days of [his] life," so, too, may all the days of my life be filled with a singular longing for you.

Don't Waste Your Time

Look carefully then how you walk, not as
unwise but as wise, making the best use
of the time, because the days are evil.
Ephesians 5:15-16

Life is made up of time: days, weeks, months, years, decades. What a shame to waste our days in worry and despair. God wants more for us. He still wants to use us for his purposes. The days *are* evil and there is work for us to do. Live every day for the assignment God has given you—even if that assignment is simply saying quiet prayers for others. Blessed are those whom God calls to be intercessors.

Father, you have me here on earth for a reason. You have a divine assignment for me during these evil days. I pray for a positive vision of that assignment, along with the will and energy to fulfill it. Lord, time is such a precious gift! Let me not waste one single day. Renew my energy so I can be about your business. If you desire, call me to more times of concentrated prayer for others. Give me the heart of an intercessor, praying for your will to be done here on earth as it is in heaven (Matthew 6:10). I commit all to you, Lord.

COMMUNION

*He took bread, and when he had given
thanks, he broke it and gave it to them,
saying, "This is my body, which is given for
you. Do this in remembrance of me."*

LUKE 22:19

In instituting the Lord's Supper, Jesus gave us something to do in remembrance of him. The bread represents his broken body, and the wine represents his blood.

Try to partake of the Lord's Supper soon, and do so in remembrance of the lover of your soul.

Lord, I believe there is healing in the atonement. The body of your Son was broken for me. His blood was shed for me. As I partake of his body and blood during communion, I remember him and his love for me—even in the midst of my darkest days. Thank you for the sacrifice of your Son.

Drink Deeply

Come, everyone who thirsts,
come to the waters;
and he who has no money,
come, buy and eat!
Come, buy wine and milk
without money and without price.

Isaiah 55:1

God's gifts to us are *free*. Our earthly life was given to us freely. Our eternal life is based solely on our faith in Christ's sacrifice. We have only to receive these gifts...and drink deeply.

Father, the spiritual riches you have provided for me never cease to astonish me. I can come to you thirsty, and be filled. I can come as I am, without anything with which to pay for your blessings. I can come, buy, and eat freely. I can drink deeply of your riches from a well that never runs dry. Lord, in the face of my cancer, your spring still pours forth refreshing waters for my thirsty soul. Thank you.

DWELLING SECURELY IN
THE WILDERNESS

I will make with them a covenant of
peace and banish wild beasts from the
land, so that they may dwell securely in
the wilderness and sleep in the woods.
EZEKIEL 34:25

In the land of cancer, wild beasts roam—beasts of fear, pain, anxiety, and depression. But all of these beasts and more, God will banish. He has made a covenant of peace with us so that we can dwell securely. We can sleep safely in the dark woods.

Lord, you are a covenant-keeping God. Your promises are solid. And you have said you will banish the wild beasts from my land and enable me to dwell securely in this wilderness. You will see to it that I can sleep safely in the woods. For all this, I praise and thank you, Lord. I praise you that I can rest securely in your promises.

Avoiding Stress

Cast your burden on the LORD,
and he will sustain you;
he will never permit
the righteous to be moved.
PSALM 55:22

Stress while undergoing cancer is not helpful. It only puts more strain on our immune system. When we feel stressed, we must learn to cast our burden on the Lord, trusting him to sustain us.

Dear Lord, my burdens are many. Cancer has a way of multiplying my trials. Father, I pray you will never permit me to be moved in my faith. Keep me strong as I cast my burdens on you. Please relieve my stress and replace it with peace. Sustain me, Lord, in my daily battle to be well again. Give me wisdom to ration my energy, saving it for the things that really matter.

Every Life Has Value

Are not two sparrows sold for a penny? And
not one of them will fall to the ground apart
from your Father. But even the hairs of your
head are all numbered. Fear not, therefore;
you are of more value than many sparrows.
Matthew 10:29-31

The value of a human life, from God's point of view, is immeasurable. We are worth much to God. Each of us.

Lord, thank you for being my caring Father. Thank you for the inestimable value you place on my life. You watch when a sparrow falls to the ground, and you number the hairs on my head—before and after chemo. You created this universe, and yet you also fashioned me. You know my name. You care for me. You know my comings and goings.

Lord, I pray that in your careful watch over me, you will see my present distress and bring healing to my body. This sparrow looks to you for help.

SELF-CARE

*He said to them, "Come away by yourselves
to a desolate place and rest a while."*
MARK 6:31

Looking after ourselves, especially when battling cancer, is a must. We need to follow the recommendations of our doctors; we need to eat nourishing foods and avoid stress. Part of taking care of ourselves also means knowing when we must rest. We must learn to say no when saying yes will only stress us.

Lord, thank you for inviting me to come away to a quiet spot and rest. I know you were speaking to your original disciples in today's verse, but I also know I'm a disciple too. Bring me often to the place of rest where my body and mind release their stress, and where I can refresh and recharge my batteries. Lord, help me not take on too much responsibility as I recuperate. May I learn when to say yes and when to say no—even to worthwhile activities that are simply not my calling.

PRAY IT FORWARD

*Call to me and I will answer you, and will tell you
great and hidden things that you have not known.*
JEREMIAH 33:3

A cancer diagnosis does not rob us of our tomorrows. Only passive resignation does that.

Start praying for your tomorrows, while not neglecting your todays. God has "great and hidden things" to show you. Call on him today about tomorrow. Pray it forward.

God, my future is in your hands. You hold my tomorrows. I call on you and ask for "great and hidden things" that I have not known. Lord, do not let this cancer rob me of the future you have for me. Bring each of the tomorrows you've planned for me into being. May each one be blessed by your presence. Thank you for every day and the hope of every tomorrow.

HOPE, PATIENCE, PRAYER

Rejoice in hope, be patient in
tribulation, be constant in prayer.
ROMANS 12:12

As we're "constant in prayer," we can also "rejoice in hope" and be patient during the tribulation of cancer. Hope, patience, and prayer are lifelines as we endure the battle.

If these three areas are presently weak links in your life, take time to replenish each one: your hope, your patience, and your prayer life.

Lord, thank you for hearing my many prayers during this cancer season. I praise you for your attentiveness to my needs. I rejoice in the hope that you are with me every day in this cancer battle. But as much as I try to be patient, it's often hard. Help me have a long-term view of what's ahead, patiently relying on you to get me where you want me to be. Father, as I see my patience waning or my hope failing or my prayers faltering, help me renew these parts of my life. Help me overcome.

THE COMFORTER HAS COME

*I will pray the Father, and he shall give you another
Comforter, that he may abide with you for ever.*
JOHN 14:16 KJV

God knew that each one of us would need a comforter to get through this life. Those of us traveling through the cancer valley have learned just how important comfort from another is—especially from our heavenly Father.

O Holy Spirit, thank you for your daily presence in my life. You accomplish many things for me, but I'm especially grateful for your comfort in this moment. I pray for a real sense of your presence on my hardest days. I pray for the peace only you can give. I also pray for a Holy Spirit-inspired hope for my future. Be present with me now.

Healing Humor

A joyful heart is good medicine,
but a crushed spirit dries up the bones.
PROVERBS 17:22

Laughter is a great supplement to our cancer care. We must find the humor in our situation, even when it's hard. Let's give humor a place on our support team and enjoy its presence as often as we can.

God, you know how I love to laugh. Cancer sure can put a damper on my funny bone, though. I pray you'll show me glimpses of heavenly humor, so I can laugh at some of the little things that happen during my treatment. God, bring a smile to my face daily. I want to be more cheerful as I make my way through this cancer valley. Lord, I could take a double dose of humor just about now.

CHOOSING JOY

*Though you have not seen him, you love
him. Though you do not now see him, you
believe in him and rejoice with joy that
is inexpressible and filled with glory.*
1 PETER 1:8

Joy is essential as we fight cancer. Otherwise, we're not only suffering from a physical disease, but we have no strength with which to maintain our spiritual-emotional balance when we need it most. Choose joy in the midst of cancer.

Lord, though I have not seen you, I can say I love you. I rejoice in you and receive your inexpressible joy, filled with glory. I choose joy as my emotional booster during this rough time. I choose to reject the worry and sadness that try to rob me of joy. Fill me afresh, Lord. Give me even more of your joy.

Resist the Devil

Submit yourselves therefore to God.
Resist the devil, and he will flee from you.
James 4:7

During this cancer season, the devil—our enemy—finds many ways to bring us down. Worry, predictions about the future, accusations about the cause of our cancer...all of these are lies with which he wants to torment us. Resist him!

God, the devil is trying to use this cancer as a means of bringing me down spiritually. Stand with me, Lord, as I resist his attempts to steal my joy, rob me of my future, and accuse you of not caring about me. I submit to you, knowing that as I do, the enemy must flee.

I pray that Satan will not have any place in my life. I resist him in the name of the Lord Jesus Christ and will not listen to his accusations about why I have this cancer. Strengthen me as I resist Satan in the future, knowing he will continue his attempts to bring me down.

RUNNING YOUR RACE

Since we are surrounded by so great a cloud
of witnesses, let us also lay aside every weight,
and sin which clings so closely, and let us run
with endurance the race that is set before us.

HEBREWS 12:1

Having cancer is like participating in a long-distance race. How long, we wonder, can we endure the treatments, the suspense, and the nagging wonder at our prognosis? The answer is, we can endure as long as necessary with God strengthening us. We may run slowly on many days, but we do move ahead little by little as we follow his lead.

Lord, I lay aside the weight of worry and the subtle sins that cling to me. With you empowering me, I run this endurance race looking fully to Jesus, the perfecter of my faith (Hebrews 12:2). I take his joy as my joy, his strength as my strength, his power to endure suffering as my own power to endure cancer. Lord, help me run my cancer race with bold hope. I pray you'll grant me favor to live my life in full, not missing one day of your will for me here on earth.

SILENCE

For God alone, O my soul, wait in silence,
for my hope is from him.
PSALM 62:5

Amid the clamor, we must set aside a time for silence in the presence of the Lord, in whom we have placed our hope.

Father, for you alone, I wait in silence. Refresh me daily in your presence. Restore my hope and lengthen my days.

In this time of silence, I listen for you, Lord. Speak to me words of comfort. Speak to me of your intense love for me. Tell me again of the hope I have in you because of Christ. In this silence, also, I pray you will continue to tend to my ailing body. May each cancerous cell be devoured by my selected treatment, directed by your superior hand. Intervene, Lord, in this attack on my body. Restore me, I pray.

HEALING WORSHIP

Oh come, let us worship and bow down;
let us kneel before the LORD, our Maker!
PSALM 95:6

Worship your Lord today. There will be healing for your spirit...and maybe some healing for your body as well. Begin with just a few words of praise. Perhaps the words to an old hymn. Search a hymnal or the Internet for songs of praise you can send up as a worship offering to the Lord. For starters, how about this popular stanza by Thomas Ken written in the seventeenth century? Most know it as the Doxology, but it's only one of fourteen stanzas from Ken's "Morning Hymn."

Sing it to the Lord. Then once more. Then give thanks to God for today.

Praise God, from Whom all blessings flow;
Praise Him, all creatures here below;
Praise Him above, ye heav'nly host;
Praise Father, Son, and Holy Ghost.

EXPECTING GOD'S WILL FOR *You*

Come now, you who say, "Today or tomorrow we
will go into such and such a town and spend a year
there and trade and make a profit"— yet you do
not know what tomorrow will bring. What is your
life? For you are a mist that appears for a little time
and then vanishes. Instead you ought to say,
"If the Lord wills, we will live and do this or that."

JAMES 4:13-15

It's comforting to know God has a will for our lives.
His will, not ours. No person on the planet is guaran-
teed tomorrow. We are blessed to have each new day—
as those of us with cancer are well aware. And although
Scripture teaches we're merely a mist that appears
briefly and then vanishes, we must remember we are
God's mist and he cares for us deeply.

Father, I realize how brief life is. Not just my life, but
everyone's. I have no guarantee about tomorrow, but I
do have today, and I thank you for this one day. Tomorrow I will rejoice in yet another 24-hour gift, should it
be granted to me. Lord, thank you for loving me and for
having a perfectly designed will for me. Truly, I will live
and "do this or that" as a recipient of your grace.

AVOID NEGATIVITY

Whatever is true, whatever is honorable,
whatever is just, whatever is pure, whatever
is lovely, whatever is commendable, if there
is any excellence, if there is anything worthy
of praise, think about these things.

PHILIPPIANS 4:8

Negative thinking does us no good. It can't destroy even one cancer cell. Instead, let's think on what's good and honorable—all things worthy of praise.

Lord, I turn my mind away from all the negative distractions around me. I won't entertain destructive thoughts that attack my mind. Help me, Father, by reminding me of some of the many good and commendable things on which I can dwell. Help me as I align my thinking with uplifting thoughts that may very well impact my body in a healing way. Lord, I turn my mind toward you, now and every day.

Healthy Living

*Do you not know that your body is a temple of
the Holy Spirit within you, whom you have
from God? You are not your own, for you were
bought with a price. So glorify God in your body.*
1 Corinthians 6:19-20

For many of us, our cancer may be related to our lifestyle: our eating and exercise habits, our stress levels, and other choices we've made. We can't undo the past, but we can change the present by eating more living foods (fruits and vegetables), cutting out junk food, reducing causes of stress in our life, and eliminating any other bad habits we've acquired. Even little changes can help.

God, in some ways I've not been kind to my body. As I pray for healing and heed my doctors' advice, I also pray you'll help me alter my lifestyle. Help me choose the nutritious foods my body needs. Help me turn away from stress. Show me ways to get exercise that I'll actually do and that will revive my energy level rather than tax it. Lord, I need guidance in living a different kind of life. Help me honor this earthly body you've given me.

SETTING GOALS

One thing I do: forgetting what lies behind
and straining forward to what lies ahead,
I press on toward the goal for the prize of
the upward call of God in Christ Jesus.
PHILIPPIANS 3:13-14

I f we see our cancer as a dead end in our life, we may hinder healing. Instead, let's look ahead to a better future. Let's press on toward the goal God has for us. Let's plan to live.

What's on your bucket list? What do you think *God* would put on your bucket list? Plan for it.

Dear Father, I'm hoping for much more out of life. I don't want to give up what you've given me. I want more, Lord. I want to enjoy more days and accomplish more of what you have planned for me. Help me to be full of hope, not discouragement, as I strain forward to what lies ahead. Give me some realistic goals I can pursue in a designated time frame. Lord, whatever you have for me to do in this life, bring it on!

THE GOD OF ALL POWER

Yours, O LORD, is the greatness and the
power and the glory and the victory and the
majesty, for all that is in the heavens and in
the earth is yours. Yours is the kingdom,
O LORD, and you are exalted as head above all.
1 CHRONICLES 29:11

Take time to recall God's greatness in light of your cancer. Remind yourself of his power, along with the glory and victory and majesty of all that belongs to him. His is the kingdom. Look outside and marvel at his creation—whether the mountains, the sea, the sky with its clouds, the stars at night, or the seasonal colors. All these and more he has made for us.

Hallelujah, Lord! How great a God you are! Yours is the greatness and the power and the glory and the majesty. All that is in heaven and on earth is yours! O Lord, yours is the kingdom, and you are indeed exalted as head above all. Father, I give you praise for your strength. I worship you for your majesty and beauty. I revel in your love and care for me. Praise belongs to you, O God!

"TEACH US TO
NUMBER OUR DAYS"

*So teach us to number our days
that we may get a heart of wisdom.*
PSALM 90:12

A cancer diagnosis has a way of reminding us of how short our days on earth are. We are wise to allow our cancer to remind us why we're here and to "teach us to number our days that we may get a heart of wisdom."

Father God, though I hate this cancer, I'm grateful that it reminds me of the importance of numbering and treasuring my days. Lord, in so doing, may I gain a heart of wisdom. May I become wise in handling the many details that come with cancer. May wisdom guide my every decision about my treatment, and may wisdom remind me how to interact with others who ask me about my health. Lord, as I number my days, may I remember your plans for me and what I have yet to accomplish while I'm here.

NOT GUILTY

*There is therefore now no condemnation
for those who are in Christ Jesus.*

ROMANS 8:1

Some of us with cancer experience feelings of guilt. We may feel our cancer is God's payback for something in our past. Or we may feel ashamed for not being able to perform the responsibilities we feel are ours. Or we may have only a vague sense of guilt, unable to pinpoint the offense.

But God does not assign guilt to us, nor does he send cancer as punishment for our sins of the past. There is *no* condemnation for those who are in Christ Jesus. None.

Lord, thank you that Jesus bore the penalty for my sins. I praise you that I am now blameless in your sight, that the righteousness of Christ is mine. Help me overcome any lingering feelings of guilt. Keep reminding me that my cancer is not retribution from you for any previous offenses. With my past behind me, my sins forgiven, and my righteousness established in Christ, may I now focus on the future as long as you grant me breath.

Unceasing Prayer

Pray without ceasing.
1 Thessalonians 5:17

It seems impossible to pray without ceasing. But if we maintain a prayerful attitude throughout the day, we can do it...and see great results. Since we all have some sort of inward conversation going on in our heads most of the time, why not bring the Lord into it? Let that become an aspect of your praying without ceasing.

Lord, this cancer has made me more aware of my need to pray—often and in faith. Help me develop this habit of praying without ceasing, always remaining in an attitude of prayer. Remind me to bring you into every internal conversation going on in my mind. May my many concerns about this cancer be expressed as never-ending prayers.

Father, if this cancer has the effect of enlisting me as a more diligent prayer warrior, I will be grateful. May my ceaseless prayers be answered, Lord.

YOUR GLORIFIED BODY

Beloved, we are God's children now, and
what we will be has not yet appeared;
but we know that when he appears we shall be
like him, because we shall see him as he is.

1 JOHN 3:2

Whatever awaits us at the end of our cancer journey, we know that someday in eternity we shall
see God as he is and be like him. In the meantime, we
are his children now and must take the time to enjoy
being offspring of the heavenly king.

Father, what a joy it is to be your child! I accept all the
paternal blessings you send my way. Though I endure
this cancer now, I see by faith the glorified body that will
be mine when I see you as you are (Philippians 3:20-
21). Lord, such a vision diminishes the fear of cancer
remarkably. I have everlasting life to anticipate. O Lord,
to be like you—both here and in eternity—is my prayer.

WHEN YOUR
EMOTIONS ARE RAW

For everything there is a season, and a time for every
matter under heaven...a time to weep, and a time
to laugh; a time to mourn, and a time to dance.
ECCLESIASTES 3:1,4

You have turned for me my mourning into
dancing; you have loosed my sackcloth
and clothed me with gladness.
PSALM 30:11

We all want more times to laugh...and to dance. Few are the times we want to weep or mourn. Yet every emotion is likely to be tapped during our cancer days. During the hard days when our emotions are raw, it's good to know that seasons *do* pass eventually. We can hope for better times ahead—days when we can once again laugh and dance.

God, this is a hard day for me. You know the reasons my emotions are raw. You understand why I mourn, why I weep. Lord, bring me fresh strength. Renew my spirit. Turn my mourning into dancing. Loosen my sackcloth of cancer. Clothe me, Father, with gladness. I so yearn to dance once again.

YOUR BODY IS GOD'S TEMPLE

*Do you not know that you are God's temple
and that God's Spirit dwells in you?*
1 CORINTHIANS 3:16

*He who is in you is greater than
he who is in the world.*
1 JOHN 4:4

It seems odd that cancer should dwell in the same body as the Holy Spirit. But we *are* God's temple and he *does* live in us. Even more so, God within us is greater than our worldly cancer. What a glorious reality!

Holy Spirit, thank you for your presence in me. I am your temple and you are my comforter, helper, healer, guide, and so much more. Greater are you in me than this cancer that can only exist in this sin-filled world.

Lord, I pray my cancer would diminish in the presence of the Holy Spirit within me. I pray for a temple that is fully yours, with no room for disease or weakness. Lord, dwell in me now and forever. My body is your home. Greater are you than all else in this world.

GOD'S WORKMANSHIP

We are his workmanship, created in Christ
Jesus for good works, which God prepared
beforehand, that we should walk in them.
EPHESIANS 2:10

You were created by God for good works. You are God's workmanship...you are not defined by your cancer.

God, you have created me for a purpose, and you have good works for me to accomplish. *That* is my focus, Lord—not my cancer. I may *have* cancer, but I know I am not my cancer. My life is much larger than any disease that attacks me. I find my identity as your child, your workmanship. Lord, may I continue to walk in the good works you've planned for me for as long as you give me breath.

WHOLE-PERSON CHRISTIANITY

*Now may the God of peace himself sanctify
you completely, and may your whole spirit
and soul and body be kept blameless at
the coming of our Lord Jesus Christ.*

1 THESSALONIANS 5:23

Our God is Lord of our whole person—spirit, soul, and body. With our spirit, we interact with God. With our soul (our mind, will, and emotions), we interact with others. With our body, we interact with this world.

Give God reign over every part of your life.

Father, I thank you for creating me not just as a body of flesh and blood, but as a person with a spirit and soul. As I pray against the cancer attacking my body, I also pray for my spiritual life and my whole being. Lord, may you sanctify me completely and bring health to every part of my life. I give you lordship over all I am and ask for your blessing in my spirit, soul, and body. May all my interactions—with you, with others, and with this world—be sanctified by you, the God of peace.

THE DIVINE TOUCH OF MERCY

As Jesus passed on from there, two blind men
followed him, crying aloud, "Have mercy on
us, Son of David." When he entered the house,
the blind men came to him, and Jesus said to
them, "Do you believe that I am able to do this?"
They said to him, "Yes, Lord." Then he touched
their eyes, saying, "According to your faith be
it done to you." And their eyes were opened.
MATTHEW 9:27-30

Like the blind men in the Gospel of Matthew, may we follow the Lord, crying for mercy—and having faith that he is able to heal. May our eyes be opened.

Father God, you know my measure of faith. I pray for your divine touch on my body, just as the Lord Jesus touched the eyes of the blind men who begged for mercy. I, too, am in need of healing. Grant me the touch that signifies your presence. May it be a healing touch, Lord...full of mercy. May it mend not just my stricken body, but also any remaining wounds in my soul.

LEARNING TO RECEIVE

Until now you have asked nothing in my name.
Ask, and you will receive, that your joy may be full.
JOHN 16:24

God invites us to approach him and ask of him. For what reason? So we may receive, and our joy may be full. The problem is that we come up with all sorts of "buts"...

"But God won't heal *me*."

"But my faith is so small."

"But the doctor's report said..."

"But I don't deserve anything from God."

Lay all your "buts" aside and ask anyway.

Father, at the invitation of Jesus, I do ask for your blessing on my life, particularly my broken body. I set aside the many "buts" that would keep me from requesting and receiving your blessing. I ask in the name of the Lord Jesus, and I pray to experience the joy that accompanies your response. Help me to receive all you have for me, nothing lacking. Lord, I'm asking, just as you bid me to do.

PERSPECTIVE

Set your minds on things that are above,
not on things that are on earth.

COLOSSIANS 3:2

No matter the current state of our health, our minds need to be set on things above, not on the things of the world. The latter can only bring us down. Setting our minds on heavenly things uplifts us and gives us hope.

Father God, this cancer often pulls my attention away from the more important things—the things that are heavenly...from above. Forgive me for the many times my mind wanders back to earth. Help me return my thoughts to the heavenly things of life. Remind me to have the right perspective on my cancer, understanding that it, too, is an earthly annoyance that will one day pass and has no power over the things above. Keep my mind stayed on you, Lord. I know all will be well.

WHEN YOU DON'T
KNOW HOW TO PRAY

*The Spirit helps us in our weakness. For
we do not know what to pray for as we
ought, but the Spirit himself intercedes for
us with groanings too deep for words.*
ROMANS 8:26

Sometimes our cancer leaves us speechless. We can't summon up the right words to pray. We simply don't know what to ask for in our situation. But God knows. The Holy Spirit helps us in our weakness.

Lord, you know that I've prayed often about this cancer diagnosis. But sometimes my heart is heavy and the words just won't come. At such times, Father, I pray for your Holy Spirit to guide my prayers. Bring to mind the needful things for which I should ask. And when even that's too much for me to pray, I ask for the Spirit to intercede for me "with groanings too deep for words." Hear the groanings, if not my own requests—or silence. Help me pray rightly, Lord.

Gaining Wisdom

The Lord gives wisdom; from his mouth
come knowledge and understanding.
Proverbs 2:6

Dealing with cancer requires wisdom beyond our normal abilities. We are too close to our situation to appraise it rightly. But God can give us the wisdom and understanding we need.

Father, you give wisdom generously. True knowledge and understanding come from your mouth. Lord, I need that kind of wisdom as I deal with this cancer. Open my eyes and ears to see and hear the wisdom you have for me. Help my mind properly process each decision I must make. Lord, pour divine wisdom and understanding into my being.

ENDURING THE SIDE EFFECTS

The LORD sustains him on his sickbed;
in his illness you restore him to full health.
PSALM 41:3

Sometimes the treatments we must endure for our cancer seem worse than the disease itself. At such times, we need God's sustaining power. We must and can endure when he is with us. Trust him through every chemo or radiation session. Trust him through surgery. Trust him in all things. Pray for a restoration to full health.

Lord, if ever I needed your presence and power, it's now as I endure the treatment to combat this cancer. You know the side effects. You see how intense my suffering is. Lord, be with me through every round of treatment. Ease my side effects, comfort me when I'm in pain, and encourage me when my faith is shaky. Father, if possible, speed up the process and allow me to come out on the other side of these treatments in full health.

GOD IS NOT WORRIED

The Lord of hosts has sworn:
"As I have planned,
so shall it be,
and as I have purposed,
so shall it stand."
ISAIAH 14:24

God has a plan—and his plan will come to pass. This includes our battle with cancer, so we can trust him. By faith it will all turn out as he purposes.

God, your purposes will stand. This I believe. Still, I also believe your purposes are affected by my prayers and the prayers of those who love me. For that reason, I pray that my cancer will serve some purpose currently unknown to me. I pray that if there's something to be gained in this fight, that I will gain it. Lord, may your purpose stand, and may your plan bring about a good result.

TARGETING CANCER CELLS

He sent out his word and healed them,
and delivered them from their destruction.
PSALM 107:20

We have cancer because of normal cells that have rebelled and turned against us, thus becoming cancerous. The purpose of our various treatments is to search out and destroy the aberrant cells. Let's pray for success and an end to those destructive cells.

God, I believe with your power and the effective treatments of my trusted oncologists, these mutant cells can be destroyed. I reinforce every chemo, radiation, or surgical treatment with intense prayer, asking that you will use these means or your own healing power to target and destroy these toxic cells. I pray for the vast multiplication of healthy, normal cells that will take up the fight against neighboring cancer cells. God, I give you the praise for every decimated cancer cell and every regenerated healthy cell.

THE POWER OF PRAISING GOD

My lips will shout for joy,
when I sing praises to you;
my soul also, which you have redeemed.
PSALM 71:23

Praise and worship are music to God's ears. Let's shout for joy today and ring the rafters of heaven!

Lord, once again I come to you with praise on my lips. I shout for joy when I consider your power and your presence. I sing praises to you from my inner being... my soul worships and magnifies you. You are my awesome God—full of wonders, full of delights, full of power. I take refuge under your wings and thank you for my redemption and all the blessings to be found in Christ's work on the cross. Father, for all you are, I bow down and give you praise.

CALL FOR THE ELDERS

Is anyone among you sick? Let him call for the elders of the church, and let them pray over him, anointing him with oil in the name of the Lord.
JAMES 5:14

God has several different ways in which he chooses to heal: through medicine, natural means, miracles...and through the prayers of church leaders.

Who in your church is praying for you? Ask your pastor, your elders, or your church's prayer team to pray for you, anointing you with oil in the name of the Lord.

God, thank you for the different ways you heal. I pray for my church leadership. Give them the clarity of mind and the faith to pray for your will for me as I battle cancer. Remind them of the responsibility you've given them to minister to others in this way. Bless their obedience, Lord, and bring restoration.

Building Your Testimony

The man from whom the demons had gone begged that he might be with him, but Jesus sent him away, saying, "Return to your home, and declare how much God has done for you." And he went away, proclaiming throughout the whole city how much Jesus had done for him.

Luke 8:38-39

The work that God does in us, with or without cancer, is designed to be a witness to others of our great God. When God does his work in you, don't be shy in boasting about him. Freely "declare how much God has done for you."

Father, no matter what you choose to do about this cancer, I pray it will bring glory to you. I pray that as you work in me, I'll be bold enough to proclaim your goodness to all who have ears to hear. Lord, through this cancer, build a lasting testimony to your name. My lips are ready to declare your goodness to me.

GOD'S TIMING

I trust in you, O LORD;
I say, "You are my God."
My times are in your hand;
rescue me from the hand of my enemies
and from my persecutors!
PSALM 31:14-15

No matter what the doctors say, our times are in God's hands. We trust him with our lives. Our enemy, cancer, does not have the final say about our future. Only God has that power. Our doctors are given knowledge and wisdom, but they aren't God, nor are they able to discern his timing.

Lord, you are my God. In you I trust. My life is yours, and my time is in your hands. I call on you to rescue me from the hand of my cancerous enemies. I pray for insight into the options ahead of me. Father, save me fully: body, soul, and spirit. Give me the full count of days you have numbered for me. Let none of them fall short of fulfillment. Keep me safe until that final day.

FREE FROM WORRY

Which of you by being anxious can add
a single hour to his span of life?
MATTHEW 6:27

I f worry could cure our cancer, we'd all be cancer free. But the truth is that worry does nothing to change our cancer and cannot add a single hour to our life. So stop being anxious. Trust God and live.

Lord, sometimes I worry about my cancer, even though I realize this accomplishes nothing. Being anxious about the future is just a waste of precious energy. Instead, I want to trust you more and live life to the fullest. Keep me free from worry, and help me to be more trusting. Help me take my eyes off my cancer and turn my gaze to you and your perfect will for me.

Nature's Cure

God said, "Behold, I have given you every
plant yielding seed that is on the face of all
the earth, and every tree with seed in its
fruit. You shall have them for food."
GENESIS 1:29

There's much to be said about eating well in order
to restore our health. If we've been lazy about nutrition, it's time to become informed about eating living
foods that our bodies need. We must be willing to learn
new eating habits and other ways to take better care of
ourselves.

God, thank you for the food you give me daily. I pray
for a willingness to learn more about the good foods
that nourish my body and even help to fight off cancer. Lead me to good sources of information through
trusted friends, professional dietitians, or books and
authoritative Internet sites. Keep me from any sort of
quackery, Lord; lead me to wise counselors.

"But God..."

*But God will redeem my soul
from the power of the grave,
for He shall receive me.*
PSALM 49:15 NKJV

Two of the most encouraging words in the Bible are "but God." Preceding this phrase there is often troubling news. *After* these two words, though, we see God's remedy. No matter what the results of the lab tests are, just remember to add these two words: "but God."

Father, you are my great God. Nothing is too hard for you. When all else fails me...when other people let me down...when the doctor's report looks gloomy...I can always add "but God." You never fail me, Lord. You are faithful to the end. Today I pray that you would show yourself strong on my behalf. Strengthen me, encourage me, bless me with your presence. I praise you for your ongoing goodness to me in this health challenge.

CONTENTMENT

I have learned, in whatsoever state
I am, therewith to be content.
PHILIPPIANS 4:11 KJV

The apostle Paul tells us he had to *learn* to be content. He faced tremendous adversity throughout his ministry. He knew both abundance and lack. He experienced both hunger and the joy of a good meal. But when it came right down to it, his contentment was not based on his outward circumstances. It was based on trusting in God's provision (Philippians 4:12-13).

In our cancer walk, let's take the opportunity to learn contentedness.

Dear Lord, going through cancer offers many reasons to be discontent. The treatments with their harsh side effects, the ongoing tests, the uncertainty about my future, the pain the cancer causes...even with all this going on, I know I need to learn to be content and grateful for each day. I need to learn to rely on your strength. Along with contentment, I also need patience, God. Remind me during the difficult times that, like Paul, I, too, can learn contentment in my trials and in "whatsoever state" I may find myself.

CANCER CANNOT SEPARATE YOU FROM THE LOVE OF CHRIST

Who shall separate us from the love of Christ?
Shall tribulation, or distress, or persecution, or
famine, or nakedness, or danger, or sword?
ROMANS 8:35

Since nothing can separate us from the love of Christ (Romans 8:38-39), we can know and rely on the fact that our cancer does not continue without God's notice and care. He is not absent. He is here, never separating himself from us, his beloved children.

O Lord, how great it is to know that nothing can separate me from the love of Christ. *Nothing!* The love of Christ covers me, guards me, guides me, protects me, and shelters me from all the tribulation that cancer brings my way. Lord, keep in my mind's eye the image of myself *in* Jesus, unable to be separated by any disease or adversity—for the love of Christ is more powerful than any of these. And this strength is mine in you.

LIVING OUT YOUR YEARS

As your days, so shall your strength be.
DEUTERONOMY 33:25

What a comfort to know that God provides us with just enough strength for each new day. A fresh supply arrives from heaven every morning.

God, I'm thankful that I don't have to endure cancer in my own human strength, for my meager portion runs out quickly. Thank you for the divine strength you provide each new day—strength to live out my full allotment of years. Today may I feel the surge of your heavenly power in me. Be with me, Father. Impart divine strength to this ailing body.

Prayers of Thankfulness

Enter his gates with thanksgiving,
and his courts with praise!
Give thanks to him; bless his name!
Psalm 100:4

Praising God releases our worries and entrusts them to the one whom we worship. We can never over-praise God. We can always enter his gates with thanksgiving. Those gates are never closed.

Lord, I continue to praise you day after day. You're worthy of worship and exaltation. Today, I enter your gates with true thanksgiving. I come into your courts with praise. Father, I give thanks to you for all your blessings, even the ones you're working in me through this cancer fight. I bless your name. You are my worthy Lord. Praise you again and again!

No More Disease

He will wipe away every tear from their eyes,
and death shall be no more, neither shall there
be mourning, nor crying, nor pain anymore,
for the former things have passed away.

REVELATION 21:4

Having cancer makes us all the more eager to see that day when there shall be no more disease, as these "former things" will have passed away. Imagine entering a heavenly world of no cancer, no chemo, and no need for surgery. Healthy forever! That day is on its way.

Father, I long for eternity, when you shall wipe every tear from my eyes and where death shall be no more. I eagerly anticipate my arrival at the place where mourning, crying, and pain are unknown. Meanwhile, in this mortal life, I pray for comfort and healing. I pray for your presence beside me. Watch over me during this time, and bring restoration to my body. May this cancer soon be a former thing that has passed away.

The Fruit of the Spirit

*Walk by the Spirit, and you will not gratify
the desires of the flesh... The fruit of the
Spirit is love, joy, peace, patience, kindness,
goodness, faithfulness, gentleness, self-
control; against such things there is no law.*
GALATIANS 5:16,22-23

Every single fruit of God's Holy Spirit is needful as
we endure cancer. The "desires of the flesh," however, continually wage war against the ways of the Spirit.
But we have the power to choose the Spirit over the
flesh. The fruit is there for us. We must simply walk in it.

God, thank you for giving me your Holy Spirit. By faith, I
choose to walk in the power of your Spirit and not gratify the desires of my flesh. I pray to be filled with love,
joy, peace, patience, kindness, goodness, faithfulness,
gentleness, and self-control. May this fruit be mani-
fested in me as I endure cancer. May the joy of the Holy
Spirit be my steady strength. Bless me, Lord, with the
power and presence of your Spirit.

Divine Energy

Being strengthened with all power,
according to his glorious might, for all
endurance and patience with joy.
Colossians 1:11

Cancer can easily deplete our strength, leaving us physically weak and vulnerable to additional threats to our health. We must ask for and rely on the supernatural energy of God to get us through our battle and to give us endurance and patience.

Father, my body is under attack, and thus my energy is low at times. Lord, you can rejuvenate me from your abundant energy supply. Give me a fresh vitality. I pray especially for my body to be imbued with vigorous power in its war against this cancer. Lord, may you strengthen me for "all endurance and patience," according to your glorious might.

THE PRESENCE OF THE LORD

In your presence there is fullness of joy;
at your right hand are pleasures forevermore.
PSALM 16:11

We need constant reminders of God's unfailing presence during our cancer fight. Daily interruptions distract our mind from the peace of knowing God is with us—but we need to embrace the fullness of joy his presence brings.

God, in your presence is the fullness of joy I long for right now. Your right hand holds pleasures forevermore. As I've asked before, so I continue to ask for your presence to be with me as I go through this battle with cancer. May your joy ease my mind and strengthen my resolve. May this sense of well-being you offer also work toward the healing of my body. Lord, I take great comfort in your presence.

GOD IS REJOICING OVER YOU

The LORD your God is in your midst,
a mighty one who will save;
he will rejoice over you with gladness;
he will quiet you by his love;
he will exult over you with loud singing.

ZEPHANIAH 3:17

Not only is the presence of God with us, but he is mighty to save *and* he rejoices over us with gladness. He quiets us with his love.

Imagine God exulting over you today with loud singing. I can hear it...can you?

O God, thank you for not only providing your presence here in the midst of my turmoil, but also for being mighty to save, no matter the problem. Yes, you are bigger and more powerful than this cancer. You rejoice over me during this time with gladness. You quiet me with your love—and best of all, I can hear you exulting over me with loud singing. Praise you, Lord!

Glorifying God in Illness

When Jesus heard it he said, "This illness does not lead to death. It is for the glory of God, so that the Son of God may be glorified through it."

John 11:4

It's interesting that Jesus spoke of illness that does not lead to death, but to the glory of God. How can illness glorify him?

We can magnify God in our suffering when we humbly approach him and ask for his healing touch. Then we must trust him for all that follows, allowing him to be glorified by our illness in any way he chooses.

Lord, you know that cancer kills people. It's a horrible, destructive, evil attack on my body. However, despite its threat, I can take comfort in knowing that not all illness leads to death, but some is used by you so that your Son may be glorified through it. God, I pray that will be my case. Surely coming out the other side of this cancer battle in restored health will be to your glory. Lord, how that happens—whether through the protocol my oncologist recommends or through your divine touch—doesn't really matter. And if, in your wisdom, this cancer leads me to heaven, the praise still goes to you. Yes, Lord, may your will be accomplished in my life through this cancer.

Your Wonder-Working God

*You are the God who works wonders; you have
made known your might among the peoples.*
PSALM 77:14

God *still* works wonders. He still makes known
his might among us. God is always for us, never
against us. In our darkest hour, he sees, he hears, he
knows our pain, and he offers comfort.

Father God, you work wonders and you *are* a wonder.
You are mighty and "have made known your might
among the peoples." Lord, I pray you will work a wonder
for me in my body. Bring restoration and healing. Make
your might known in me by bringing me new health
and a strengthened immune system. Bless those
through whom you display your wonders by way of
medicine and treatments that can contribute to healing. Even then, Lord, it is your marvelous design at
work...and I praise you for it.

SEEK GOD'S PRESENCE CONTINUALLY

Seek the LORD and his strength;
seek his presence continually!
1 CHRONICLES 16:11

Though God's strength and presence are always available to us, we have to seek them to find them. In other words, all the resources we need to endure through cancer are already here with us, but we must open our eyes to see them.

Lord, I do seek you and your strength. I do so daily. I crave your presence through my cancer trial. I pray for your power and strength to see me through the pain. In seeking you, I also seek your perfect will for my life. I pursue your presence, power, and purpose. May you pour out your divine blessings on my behalf. May others who visit me and those whom I visit sense your presence and notice the peace I experience.

THE WAYS OF THE LORD

Oh, the depth of the riches and wisdom and knowledge of God! How unsearchable are his judgments and how inscrutable his ways!

ROMANS 11:33

God's wisdom is not our wisdom. His judgments are unsearchable and his ways inscrutable. But we can rest confidently in the riches and wisdom and knowledge of him who loves us.

Father, your ways are not easily known to us humans. Life was proceeding along just fine, and then came the unexpected cancer diagnosis. And yet this was no surprise to you. You are not shocked, nor even disappointed. Why? Because, Lord, your ways are workable even in the midst of cancer. No adversity halts your ability to work in my life. This is the inscrutableness of your ways. Lord, I give you praise. Oh, the depth of the riches and wisdom and knowledge you embody!

Pray Boldly

Three times I pleaded with the Lord about this [thorn in my flesh], that it should leave me. But he said to me, "My grace is sufficient for you, for my power is made perfect in weakness." Therefore I will boast all the more gladly of my weaknesses, so that the power of Christ may rest upon me.

2 Corinthians 12:8-9

Will prayer heal our cancer? That's the unspoken question we all have when our cancer journey hits a rough patch. Will we recover? Or is this God's way of taking us home?

If we can set these questions aside and simply pray with the faith we have, leaving the rest to God, we will do well. Paul prayed for deliverance from his thorn in the flesh, and God's response was to remind Paul that God's grace was sufficient to help him bear the thorn. That might be your answer too.

God, like Paul, I pray with a measure of faith for you to remove this cancer, whether through the treatments my doctor has ordered or by any other means. This cancer leaves me weakened, but I know your power is made perfect in my weakness. Still, Lord, I pray for healing. I pray for my "thorn" to be removed. If, like in Paul's case, the thorn is not removed, may I experience your sufficient grace. May your power rest on me.

THE GIFT OF LIFE

I charge you in the presence of God,
who gives life to all things.
1 TIMOTHY 6:13

Our God gives life, sustains life, and—when the time comes—ushers us into eternal life. As he presently preserves our life, we give him praise.

God, thank you for this earthly life. What a wonderful gift it is! I pray that as you have given me this life, you will also sustain it in the future until the final day you have set for me. I pray that my health will never cause me to become a burden to those I love. Strengthen my body, Lord. Revitalize my immune system. Ward off the cancer cells that have wreaked havoc in my body. As the giver of life, Father, I pray you will continue to give me life into the future.

Holy Ground

The commander of the LORD's army said to Joshua,
"Take off your sandals from your feet, for the place
where you are standing is holy." And Joshua did so.
Joshua 5:15

In our daily dealings with cancer, we often forget the concept that as Christians, we—in a very real sense—walk on holy ground every day. When we're in the oncologist's office, we're on holy ground. In the chemo room, we're on holy ground. In the radiation lab or operating room, it's all holy ground...because God is there with us.

Lord, wherever you are is holy ground. Yes, even in the places I most want to avoid. During my treatments, even though I don't always feel it, you are there with me. I pray you'll never let me take the sacredness of your presence for granted. I take off my sandals, and I stand confidently on holy ground. Lord, remind me you are here.

THE GOD WHO HEALS

*If you will diligently listen to the voice of the
LORD your God, and do that which is right in
his eyes, and give ear to his commandments
and keep all his statutes, I will put none
of the diseases on you that I put on the
Egyptians, for I am the LORD, your healer.*

EXODUS 15:26

The greatest oncologist in the world isn't going to be our true healer. No treatment will work wonders unless the God of wonders is behind it. Look to God first as "the LORD, your healer," your *Jehovah Rophe*. Consider your medical team as one of God's agents for healing—but know it's God who heals.

God, I look to you as my *Jehovah Rophe*, the God who heals. I will listen diligently to the medical team you've assigned to me, but I realize that any healing I experience will ultimately come from you. My oncologist is not my god. I pray for him to have wisdom, believing that such wisdom must come from you. Lord, you are my true oncologist in this cancer fight.

He Will Lift You Up

Be gracious to me, O LORD!
See my affliction from those who hate me,
O you who lift me up from the gates of death.

PSALM 9:13

God is a gracious God. He sees our cancerous affliction, and he lifts us from the gates of death. He never for one moment leaves us to suffer alone.

God, lift me up today. In your graciousness, see my affliction and save me. Lift me from the gates of death and bring me to the fountain of life. Refresh me with the living waters of health and healing. Draw me nearer to you, my life giver, my healer, my Lord. Fortify my body in its fight against this cancer. Raise me up, Lord.

HE IS YOUR ROCK

*The LORD is my rock and my
fortress and my deliverer,
my God, my rock, in whom I take refuge,
my shield, and the horn of my
salvation, my stronghold.*

PSALM 18:2

In times of war and trouble, we all need a place of security from which to wage our battle. That place for us is on the rock, our God. In him we take refuge.

Lord God, you are my rock, fortress, and deliverer. I take refuge in you and hold you up as my shield against the enemy. You are my stronghold in days of battle. I stand on you as I would stand on the Rock of Gibraltar. I will not lose my hold on you, Lord. You keep me safe. You keep me balanced. You keep me positive in the day of adversity. You keep me *strong*.

THE LAST ENEMY

The last enemy to be destroyed is death.
1 CORINTHIANS 15:26

*We are of good courage, and we would rather be
away from the body and at home with the Lord.*
2 CORINTHIANS 5:8

The apostle Paul wasn't afraid to call death his enemy.
But he also knew it was the *last* enemy. He believed
that to be in the presence of the Lord was far better than
remaining here on earth. Though we long for healing
and seek it daily, we know that as believers in Christ,
not even death can harm us. We have a far better future
once we pass through the gates of our last enemy.

Strive to live—God is *for* life. But never be afraid to
move to higher ground.

God, as always, I pray for more time here on earth. I
have more to accomplish. But death stalks every person
on the planet. Lord, I pray against this enemy and trust
that you will keep him at bay until my permanent home
in heaven is ready for me. Though I long to be with you,
I also long to continue with you here on earth until my
assignment is completed. Lord, may your will be done.

It's Another
"Hallelujah Day"

*I heard what seemed to be the voice of a
great multitude, like the roar of many
waters and like the sound of mighty peals
of thunder, crying out, "Hallelujah! For
the Lord our God the Almighty reigns."*
REVELATION 19:6

Every day we awake, we should sing "hallelujah" to
God. He reigns forever. One day we shall join our
voices with that great multitude in eternity. We will
offer praise to God that's like "the roar of many waters"
and "mighty peals of thunder." But why wait? Practice now.

Hallelujah, Lord! You've offered me yet another glorious day to praise you, to serve you, and to love you.
Someday I will be in that mighty throng and will blend
my voice with the millions of others who will be praising
you, shouting "hallelujah" for eternity. Lord, I begin now.
I worship you and say with all my heart, "Hallelujah!"

*If Christ lives in us, we will rejoice in everything,
and we will thank and praise the Lord. We will
say, "Hallelujah! Praise the Lord" forever.*
WATCHMAN NEE

A FINAL WORD OF ENCOURAGEMENT

At the beginning of this book, I shared my wish that these prayers would encourage you through your cancer walk. I hope that's been the case. Perhaps praying regularly about your cancer has also helped you to grow in your prayer life overall. That would be an unexpected blessing from your cancer journey.

If these prayers have helped you, and if your cancer is not yet in remission, I'd like to suggest that you start over and go through them again. Also, consider passing along a copy of this book to someone you know who is fighting cancer too. Give them your copy if you're finished with it, or purchase a copy and tuck in a greeting card. And be sure to offer your own prayers for your friend.

Now, may God bless you in your every endeavor. Savor each day God gives you breath. Rejoice in hope. Love richly.

About the Author

Nick Harrison is the author of more than a dozen books, including two additional titles in the One-Minute Prayers® series: *One-Minute Prayers® for Husbands* and *One-Minute Prayers® for Dads*. His other books include *Magnificent Prayer, Power in the Promises, His Victorious Indwelling,* and *Promises to Keep: Daily Devotions for Men Seeking Integrity*. Nick and his wife, Beverly—an avid quilter—live in Oregon. Nick's website and blog can be found at nickharrisonbooks.com

Other Books You May Enjoy...

Hope in the Face of Cancer, *Amy Givler, MD*
Amy Givler, a cancer survivor, shares her experience and the stories of others with the voice of encouragement, faith, and strength she so desperately needed at the point of her diagnosis. With medical knowledge and insight, Dr. Givler offers answers and hope as she discusses

- looking at cancer through the lens of hope
- making decisions for treatment
- drawing closer to God along the journey
- facing and relating to family and friends

Dr. Givler shares more than professional wisdom; she provides comfort during an experience that too often is mired in uncertainty, fear, and loneliness.

God, I Need Your Comfort, *Kay Arthur*
Kay Arthur invites those who hurt and long for peace to be filled by the comfort of Psalm 23. As she leads readers through the reassuring promises of this beloved psalm, they will discover:

- God is present in the darkest times
- No problem is bigger than God's sufficiency
- The Lord sees and tends to every need

This gift of comfort will wrap every heart in the provision of the Great Shepherd.

To learn more about Harvest House books and
to read sample chapters, visit our website:

www.harvesthousepublishers.com

HARVEST HOUSE PUBLISHERS
EUGENE, OREGON